MW00851983

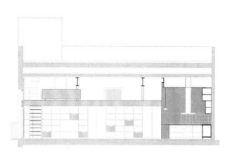

SMALL LOFTS

KÖNEMANN

© 2018 koenemann.com GmbH
www.koenemann.com

ÉDITIONS
PLACE DES
VICTOIRES

© 2018 Éditions Place des Victoires
6, rue du Mail – 75002 Paris,
pour la présente édition.
www.victoires.com
Dépôt légal : 3ᵉ trimestre 2018
ISBN : 978-2-8099-1568-6

booq
publishing

Editorial coordinator: Claudia Martínez Alonso
Art director: Mireia Casanovas Soley
Editors: Oriol Magrinyà-Go Books! Editorial; Eva Serra Agudo
Translators: Thinking Abroad

booq affirms that it possesses all the necessary rights for the publication
of this material and has duly paid all royalties related to the authors' and
photographers' rights. **booq** also affirms that is has violated no property
rights and has respected common law, all authors' rights and other rights
that could be relevant. Finally, **booq** affirms that this book contains neither
obscene nor slanderous material.
The total or partial reproduction of this book without the authorization of the
publishers violates the two rights reserved; any use must be requested
in advance.
In some cases it might have been impossible to locate copyright owners of
the images published in this book. Please contact the publisher if you are the
copyright owner in such a case.

Printed in China by Shenzhen Hua Xin Colour-printing & Platemaking Co., Ltd

ISBN 978-3-7419-2104-9

Possibly, the first image that comes to mind when we think of a loft is an open space, with very few or no walls; it is a large transparent area, with light being a key element, and it is the outcome of a clear intention to reflect the personality of its inhabitants.

There is no doubt that this type of housing originated in 1950s New York, when people began to remodel large industrial buildings that had been left empty and unused. This history has placed its mark on the main characteristics of lofts: they usually involve architectural solutions that rely on the historic structure and reinterpret it, at least partially, based on the needs and tastes of their owners.

From decidedly minimalist options that banish everything that is not essential and, above all, everything that is not functional; to proposals that seek to highlight their original, clearly industrial, elements by juxtaposing them against modern furniture, often custom-made for that space; with a view to creating, as a direct result of this very contrast, a seamless fit.

Their ultimate aim is to imbue each space with its own, clearly recognizable character. It is worth remembering that within the impersonality of the modern city, the loft, which is essentially an urban construction, is an ideal way of converting one's own home to a unique space that reflects and extends the personality of those who dwell there.

But, what happens when the available space is limited? Can the spirit of the loft be attained in just a few square meters of living space?

The intention of this book is to demonstrate that not only is it possible, but also that often these compact solutions can stand on their own in comparison with the enormous lofts of London or Manhattan. This is indeed a challenge for architects, since they must put into play all their ingenuity, technique, and talent to achieve this: gaining space by taking advantage of high ceilings; installing glass panels or sliding doors, which open up the space without sacrificing privacy; choosing a light palette of colors, enhanced with highly individual decorative elements; making the most of natural light; almost obsessively pursuing practicality without sacrificing esthetics– all of these are a constant in the projects that we have selected.

And even though most of them are under 100 square meters, all of them demonstrate how it is possible to convert what could be a small apartment into a spacious loft. This is achieved by using great care in the design and selecting finishes that divert our attention from the space limitations.

Unter Umständen ist das erste Bild, das uns in den Sinn kommt, wenn wir an einen Loft denken, das Bild eines großzügigen Raumes mit sehr wenigen oder fast gar keinen Wänden; ein großer offener Bereich, in dem das Licht die Hauptrolle spielt und der die Persönlichkeit seiner Bewohner widerspiegeln soll.

Zweifellos hat der Ursprung dieser Art von Wohnstätten, als man in den fünfziger Jahren in New York anfing, leerstehende und nicht genutzte Fabrikhallen umzuwandeln, dessen grundlegende Merkmale geprägt. Fast immer stoßen wir auf architektonische Lösungen, die auf der ehemaligen Struktur beruhen, um sie teilweise oder ganz im Einklang mit den Anforderungen und dem Geschmack der Eigentümer neu zu interpretieren.

Von eindeutig minimalistischen Optionen, bei denen alles, was nicht wesentlich – und vor allem funktionell – ist, beseitigt wird, bis hin zu Vorschlägen, die darauf abzielen, die ursprünglichen, eindeutig gewerblich geprägten Elemente hervorzuheben und sie mit modernen Möbeln konfrontiert, die für diesen Raum häufig nach Maß angefertigt wurden, damit sie sich ausgerechnet mithilfe von Kontrasten darin integrieren.

Die letzte Absicht ist, jedem Raum einen eigenen und eindeutig erkennbaren Charakter zu verleihen. Und es darf nicht vergessen werden, dass innerhalb der Unpersönlichkeit, welche uns die moderne Stadt häufig auferlegt, ein Loft (im Wesentlichen eine städtische Bauweise) die geeignete Form ist, um die Wohnstätte in einen einzigartigen Raum zu verwandeln, als Reflexion und Erweiterung der Persönlichkeit seiner Bewohner.

Doch was geschieht, wenn der vorhandene Platz begrenzt ist? Lässt sich der Geist eines Lofts auf wenigen Quadratmetern umsetzen?

In diesem Buch haben wir versucht zu zeigen, dass Lösungen nicht nur möglich sind, sondern häufig keinesfalls die riesigen Lofts in London oder Manhattan beneiden müssen. Eine Situation, die zur einer Herausforderung für den Architekten wird, da sie von ihm verlangt, sein ganzes Einfallsreichtum, seine Technik und sein Talent ins Spiel zu bringen, um dies zu erreichen: Von der Ausnutzung der Deckenhöhe, um Raum zu gewinnen, bis hin zum Einsatz von Glasverkleidungen oder Schiebetüren, dank denen durchscheinende Bereiche erzielt werden, ohne dabei auf Privatsphäre zu verzichten; der Einsatz einer Palette von hellen Farben, angereichert mit dekorativen Elementen mit großartiger Persönlichkeit; die maximale Ausnutzung von Tageslicht und eine fast besessenen Suche nach dem Praktischen, ohne auf Ästhetik zu verzichten... all diese Lösungen sind eine Konstante bei den Projekten, die wir ausgewählt haben.

Und obgleich die überwiegende Mehrheit unter 100 m² groß ist, sehen wir in allen, wie sich das, was eine kleine Wohnung sein könnte, in einen großzügigen Loft verwandelt, mit einer äußerst gepflegten Gestaltung und dem letzten Schliff, die uns die Beschränkung des Raumes vergessen lassen.

Il est possible que la première image qui nous vienne à l'esprit lorsque nous pensons à un loft soit celle d'un vaste espace, avec très peu voire aucun mur ; un grand espace ouvert avec la lumière comme élément phase et une volonté très claire de refléter la personnalité de ses occupants.

L'origine de ce type d'habitation a été sans aucun doute marquée par ses principales caractéristiques lorsque dans les années 50 à New York les entrepôts industriels laissés vides et hors d'usage ont commencé à être transformés : nous nous trouvons pratiquement toujours face à des solutions architectoniques qui reposent sur l'ancienne structure afin de la réaménager partiellement ou entièrement selon les besoins et les goûts des propriétaires.

D'un point de vue clairement minimaliste qui retire tout ce qui est inutile et surtout fonctionnel jusqu'aux propositions qui recherchent la mise en valeur des éléments d'origine, clairement industriels, en les confrontant à du mobilier moderne réalisé sur mesure pour cet espace, à la recherche de leur intégration notamment grâce au contraste.

La dernière intention est de donner à chaque espace son caractère propre et clairement reconnaissable. Sans oublier que dans l'impersonnalité qu'impose souvent la ville moderne, le loft (construction essentiellement urbaine) est une manière idéale de transformer sa propre habitation en un espace unique et singulier, reflet et extension de la personnalité de ses occupants.

Que faire lorsque l'espace disponible est limité ? Est-il possible d'obtenir l'esprit loft dans quelques mètres ?

Ce livre tente de montrer que non seulement cela est possible, mais que bien souvent les solutions n'ont rien à envier aux grands lofts de Londres ou de Manhattan. Une situation qui devient un défi pour l'architecte, car cela nécessite de mettre en jeu toute son ingéniosité, sa technique et son talent pour y parvenir : de la maximisation de la hauteur des plafonds pour gagner de l'espace à l'utilisation des panneaux en verre ou des portes coulissantes qui permet d'obtenir des pièces ouvertes sans pour autant renoncer à l'intimité ; l'utilisation d'une palette de couleurs claires, riche en éléments de décoration avec une forte personnalité ; l'exploitation au maximum de la lumière naturelle et une recherche presque obsessionnelle du côté pratique sans pour autant renoncer à l'esthétique... toutes ces solutions sont une constante dans les projets sélectionnés.

Même si la plupart d'entre eux sont inférieurs à 100 m², on remarque dans tous, ce que pourrait être un petit appartement transformé en un vaste loft, avec un design très soigné et des finitions faisant oublier l'espace limité.

Posiblemente, la primera imagen que nos viene a la cabeza cuando pensamos en un loft es la de un amplio espacio, con muy pocas o sin apenas paredes; una gran zona diáfana, con la luz como protagonista y con una voluntad clarísima de reflejar la personalidad de sus habitantes.

Sin duda, los orígenes de este tipo de vivienda, cuando en los años 50 en Nueva York se empezaron a reconvertir naves industriales que habían quedado vacías y en desuso, han marcado sus características principales: casi siempre nos hallamos ante soluciones arquitectónicas que se apoyan en la antigua estructura para reinterpretarla parcial o completamente de acuerdo con las necesidades y los gustos de los propietarios.

Desde opciones claramente minimalistas, en las que se elimina todo lo que no sea esencial y, sobre todo, funcional, hasta propuestas en las que se busca resaltar los elementos originales, claramente industriales, confrontándolos con un mobiliario moderno, que a menudo se ha hecho a medida para aquel espacio, buscando que se integre en él, precisamente, mediante el contraste.

La intención última es dotar a cada espacio de un carácter propio y claramente reconocible. Y es que no hay que olvidar que dentro de la impersonalidad que a menudo impone la ciudad moderna, el loft (construcción esencialmente urbana) es una forma idónea de convertir la propia vivienda en un espacio único y singular, como un reflejo y una extensión de la personalidad de sus habitantes.

¿Pero, qué sucede cuando la cantidad de espacio disponible es limitada? ¿Es posible conseguir el espíritu loft en pocos metros?

En este libro hemos intentado mostrar que no solo es posible, sino que a menudo las soluciones no tienen nada que envidiar a los enormes lofts de Londres o Manhattan. Una situación que se convierte en un reto para el arquitecto, ya que le exige poner en juego todo su ingenio, técnica y talento, para lograrlo: desde el aprovechamiento de la altura de los techos para ganar espacio al espacio hasta el uso de paneles de cristal o puertas correderas, que permiten obtener áreas diáfanas sin renunciar, a su vez, a la intimidad; la utilización de una paleta de colores clara, enriquecida con elementos decorativos con gran personalidad; el aprovechamiento al máximo de la luz natural y una búsqueda casi obsesiva de la practicidad sin renunciar a la estética... todas estas soluciones son una constante en los proyectos que hemos seleccionado.

Y aunque la inmensa mayoría está por debajo de los 100 m², en todos vemos como lo que podría ser un pequeño apartamento se convierte en un amplio loft, con un diseño muy cuidado y con acabados que nos hacen olvidar la limitación de espacio.

TINY LOFT

45 m² | 484.2 sq ft

~~~~~~~~~

BERIOT BERNARDINI ARQUITECTOS

~~~~~~~~~

MADRID, SPAIN

~~~~~~~~~

© YEN CHEN

The plan for this apartment was to make over this small space completely with a view to maximizing the space and its functionality. The bathroom and kitchen are positioned under the mezzanine, freeing up the rest to be used as the day zone. The stairway leading to the loft is placed against the partition wall in a single flight; the space underneath is used for storage. The only window onto the street is replaced by a large sliding sheet of wood, which, when the door is completely opened, transforms the balcony into a small terrace.

In dieser sehr kleinen Wohnung ist ein Komplettumbau vorgesehen, um den Raum und dessen funktionale Anwendungen zu maximieren. Unter dem Zwischengeschoss werden Toilette und Küche platziert, wodurch der Rest als Wohn- und Aufenthaltsbereich frei wird. Die Zugangstreppe zum Zwischengeschoss lehnt sich an einem Stück gegen die Scheidewand, wodurch der Raum darunter als Stauraum genutzt werden kann. Das einzige Fenster, das der Straße zugewandt ist, wird durch einen Schiebeflügel aus Holz ersetzt, der den Balkon in eine kleine Terrasse verwandelt, wenn die Tür ganz geöffnet wird.

Cette habitation, à la taille très réduite, a été entièrement rénovée afin de maximiser l'espace et ses fonctionnalités. En dessous de la mezzanine se trouvent les toilettes et la cuisine laissant le reste pour l'espace de vie. L'escalier donnant sur la mezzanine est placé contre le mur médian d'un seul pan offrant ainsi des rangements en dessous de celui-ci. La seule fenêtre qui donne sur la rue est remplacée par un grand panneau coulissant en bois qui transforme le balcon en une petite terrasse lorsque la porte est complètement ouverte.

En esta vivienda, de tamaño muy reducido, se plantea una reforma completa para maximizar el espacio y sus usos funcionales. Bajo el altillo se sitúan aseo y cocina, liberando el resto como zona de día. La escalera de acceso a altillo se dispone contra la pared medianera en un solo tramo, aprovechando para el almacenamiento el espacio bajo la misma. La única ventana que da a la calle se sustituye por una gran hoja corredera de madera que convierte el balcón en una pequeña terraza al abrir por completo la puerta.

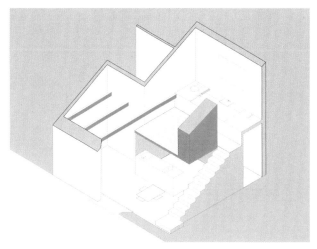

Axonometric

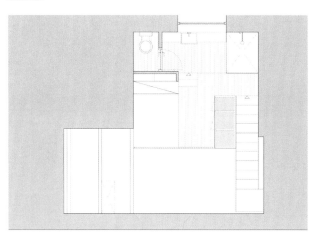

Mezzanine plan

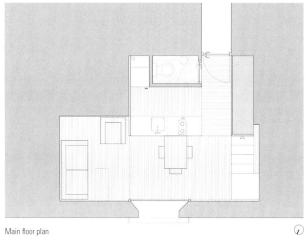

Main floor plan

The upper level is used for the private spaces, that is, the bedroom and the bath. Shelving suspended over the kitchen provides more storage space.

Man nutzt den oberen Raum aus, um eine private Nutzung für Schlafzimmer und Bad zu ermöglichen. Über der Küche hängend, ermöglicht ein Regal, Stauraum zu gewinnen.

On a tiré profit de l'espace supérieur pour disposer les espaces privatifs tels que la chambre et la salle de bains. Une étagère a été suspendue au-dessus de la cuisine afin de gagner des espaces de rangement.

Se aprovecha el espacio superior para disponer los usos privados, como son el dormitorio y el baño. Colgando sobre la cocina, se dispone de una estantería para ganar espacio de almacenamiento.

LOFT WITH
HIDDEN FURNITURE

50 m² | 538.2 sq ft

———

RUE ARQUITECTOS / RAUL MONTERO

———

PAMPLONA, SPAIN

———

© CRISTINA NÚÑEZ BAQUEDANO

The starting point for this project was a small, very compartmentalized apartment with poor lighting and ventilation. The goal was to create an open area in the center of the apartment. Careful thought was given to the array of materials that would be used: cement-bonded particle board on the new facing surfaces; ash boards on floors and ceilings; brick in a pre-existing wall; and, painstakingly refurbished, the original structural beams.

Der Ausgangspunkt beim Umbau dieser kleinen Wohnung ist ein extrem in Bereiche aufgegliederter Raum mit unzulänglichen Zuständen in puncto Beleuchtung und Belüftung. In der Mitte der Wohnung soll ein durchscheinender Bereich geschaffen werden. Die Palette an Materialien, die eingesetzt werden sollen, wurde dabei besonders bedacht: Holzzementplatten an allen neuen Frontseiten, Eschenholz für Böden und Decken. Der Freilegung der Balken der Tragewerks und einer bereits existierenden Backsteinwand wurde besondere Sorgfalt gewidmet.

Le point de départ des travaux dans ce petit appartement est un espace extrêmement divisé et peu de luminosité et d'aération. On a cherché à créer un espace ouvert au centre de l'habitation. On a pris en considération la palette de matériaux à utiliser en recourant à des panneaux de bois-ciment pour toutes les façades, un parquet en bois de frêne pour les sols et plafonds, avec une attention particulière pour récupérer les poutres de la structure, ainsi qu'un mur en brique préexistant.

El punto de partida en la reforma de este pequeño apartamento es un espacio extremadamente compartimentado y con deficientes condiciones de iluminación y ventilación. Se busca crear una zona diáfana en el centro de la vivienda. Se tiene muy en cuenta la paleta de materiales a utilizar, empleando tableros de madera-cemento en todos los nuevos frentes, tarima de madera de fresno para suelos y techos, y se pone especial cuidado para recuperar las vigas de la estructura, así como un muro de ladrillo preexistente.

To free up space, the activities are moved to the perimeter of the dwelling, which is ringed by furniture that can be changed to suit the activity: sleeping, working, relaxing, socializing, or dining.

Um Raum freizugeben, wurde die Aktivität in den Umkreis der Wohnung verlegt, umgeben von einem Möbelstück, das sich je nach der Aktivität, die ausgeübt werden soll, verwandelt: schlafen, arbeiten, sich entspannen, Freunde treffen oder essen.

Pour libérer de l'espace, l'activité se déplace dans le périmètre du bien, entouré d'un meuble changeant selon l'activité à réaliser : dormir, travailler, se reposer, se réunir ou manger.

Para liberar espacio, la actividad se desplaza al perímetro de la vivienda, rodeado por un mueble cambiante en función de la actividad a realizar: dormir, trabajar, relajarse, reunirse o comer.

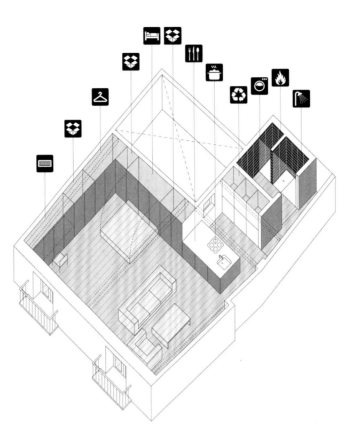

Axonometric

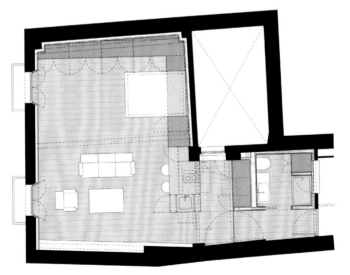

Floor plan

The completely remodeled bathroom has the
same wooden flooring as the rest of the house;
this provides a strong contrast with the black
walls and the white fixtures.

In dem komplett sanierten Bad wird der
gleiche Holzboden wie in der übrigen Wohnung
verwendet, wodurch ein starker Kontrast
zwischen dem Schwarz der Wände und dem
Weiß der der Sanitäreinrichtung geschaffen
wird.

Dans la salle de bains, entièrement refaite,
le sol en bois est le même que pour le reste
de l'habitation cherchant ainsi à créer un fort
contraste entre le noir des murs et le blanc des
sanitaires.

En el baño, completamente reformado, se
utiliza el mismo suelo de madera del resto
de la vivienda buscando un fuerte contraste
con el negro de las paredes y el blanco de los
sanitarios.

PENCIL
LOFT

59.06 m² (interior) 28.31 m² (exterior) | 35.7 sq ft (interior) 304.7 sq ft (exterior)

⸺

TERUYA KIDO / SUMA-SAGA-FUDOSAN INC.
RYOHEI TANAKA / G ARCHITECTS STUDIO

⸺

TOKYO, JAPAN

⸺

© KATSUMI HIRABAYASHI

This is a good example of an interior reconstruction in one of the 1980s Japanese "Pencil Buildings." In these tall and slender structures, such constructions became a popular way to achieve maximum profitability from minimum floor space. The main features of this renovated loft are its sloping roofs, which have been turned into a skylight that admits natural sunlight and offers a wonderful unobstructed view of the city.

Ein gutes Beispiel für die Neustrukturierung des Innenraums von Gebäuden, die in den 1980er Jahren in Japan erbaut wurden, sogenannte „Bleistift-Gebäude". Geprägt von hohen und dünnen Tragewerken, wurde diese Bauweise beliebt, um ein Höchstmaß an Rentabilität auf minimalem Raum zu erzielen. Die wichtigste Eigenschaft dieses umgebauten Lofts sind Dachschrägen, die sich in ein Oberlicht verwandeln, das den Einfall von Sonnenlicht ermöglicht und einen wundervollen Ausblick ohne Hindernisse auf die Stadt bietet.

Bon exemple de reconstruction intérieure des bâtiments créés dans les années 80 au Japon, appelés « Pencil Buildings ». Structures hautes et affinées, ces constructions se sont répandues afin d'obtenir la rentabilité maximale dans une surface au sol minimale. La principale caractéristique de ce loft rénové est les plafonds inclinés qui se transforment en une lucarne qui laisse entrer la lumière du soleil et offre une magnifique vue dégagée de la ville.

Buen ejemplo de reconstrucción interior de los edificios creados en los años 80 en Japón, los denominados "Pencil Buildings". De estructuras altas y delgadas, estas construcciones se popularizaron para conseguir la máxima rentabilidad en el mínimo espacio de suelo. La característica principal de este loft reformado son los techos inclinados, que se convierten en una claraboya que permite la entrada de la luz solar natural y ofrece una maravillosa vista sin obstáculos de la ciudad.

To bring a welcoming feel into the industrial interior of the penthouse, a painting technique reminiscent of traditional Japanese Washi paper is used on the walls and ceiling.

Um eine Harmonie zwischen dem Industriecharakter des Innenraums dieses Dachgeschosses und einer behaglichen Atmosphäre zu erzielen, wird an Wänden und Decke eine Maltechnik verwendet, die an das traditionelle japanische Washi-Papier erinnert.

Pour obtenir une harmonie entre l'intérieur industriel du dernier étage et une ambiance chaleureuse, on a recours à une technique de peinture sur murs et plafond qui rappelle le papier traditionnel japonais Washi.

Para conseguir armonía entre el interior industrial del ático con una atmósfera acogedora, se utiliza una técnica de pintura en paredes y techo que recuerda al papel tradicional japonés Washi.

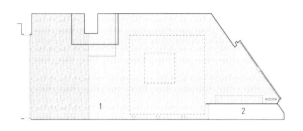

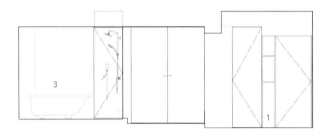

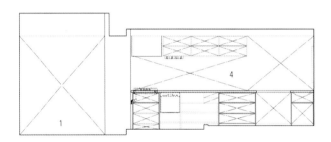

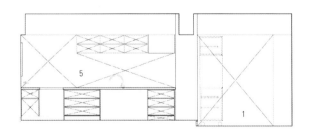

1. Entrance
2. Bedroom
3. Bathroom
4. Kitchen
5. Living room

Sections

The bathroom is in one room, near the kitchen, allowing the plumbing to be centralized; it can be hidden behind a sliding curtain.

Das Bad ist neben der Küche in eine räumliche Einheit eingebunden, wodurch sich die Leitungen zusammenfassen lassen, kann hinter einem Schiebevorhang verborgen werden.

La salle de bains s'intègre dans un cadre unique, à proximité de la cuisine, ce qui permet de réunir les canalisations et être ainsi cachée derrière un rideau coulissant.

El baño se integra en un único ambiente cerca de la cocina, lo que permite agrupar las canalizaciones, y puede ocultarse tras una cortina corredera.

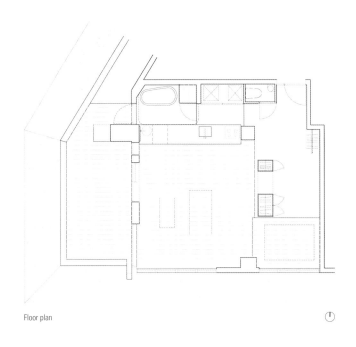

Floor plan

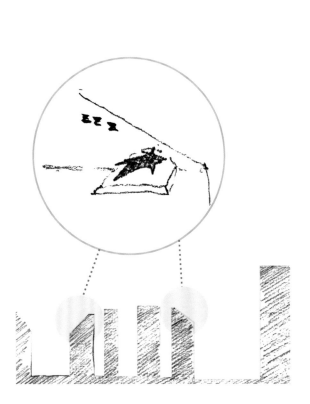

INTERLOCKING PUZZLE LOFT

60 m² | 645.83 sq ft

—

KYU SUNG WOO ARCHITECTS

—

NEW YORK, NEW YORK, UNITED STATES

—

© PAUL WARCHOL

Constructed like a jigsaw puzzle with perfectly fitting pieces, this loft makes the most of its very limited space. The design takes advantage of the extra space formed by the vaulted ceiling to create elements that are just the right size, such as the bed platform, with cupboards both above and below. The color scheme is chosen especially to go with the materials that are used. The glass partition that separates the sleeping area from the living room allows in the natural light.

Auf sehr geringem Raum wird dieser Loft als Puzzlespiel erbaut, dessen Stücke tadellos zusammenpassen, um den größtmöglichen Raum zu erzielen. Unter Ausnutzung der Gewölbedecke beschließt der Architekt, Elemente zu schaffen, die sich an diesen Höhenunterschied anpassen, wie die Plattform, die das Bett über und die Wandschränke unter sich beherbergt. Der Farbpalette wurde im Einklang mit den verwendeten Materialien eigens ausgewählt. Eine Glaswand teilt den Schlafzimmerbereich vom Wohnzimmer ab und lässt Tageslicht einfallen.

Dans un espace très réduit, ce loft est construit comme un puzzle dont les pièces s'encastrent à la perfection afin d'obtenir un vaste espace au possible. En profitant du plafond voûté, on opte pour la création d'éléments qui s'adaptent à cette dénivellation comme la plateforme qui comprend le lit et les armoires au-dessus et en dessous de celle-ci. La palette de couleurs est particulièrement bien choisie selon les matériaux utilisés. Un paravent en verre divise la partie nuit du séjour laissant ainsi passer la lumière naturelle.

En un espacio muy reducido, este loft se construye como un puzzle cuyas piezas encajan a la perfección con el fin de obtener el máximo espacio posible. Aprovechando el techo abovedado, se opta por crear elementos que se adapten a este desnivel, como la plataforma que lleva a la cama y los armarios por encima y debajo de ella. La paleta de colores está especialmente escogida acorde los materiales usados. Una mampara de cristal divide la zona de dormitorio de la sala de estar dejando pasar la luz natural.

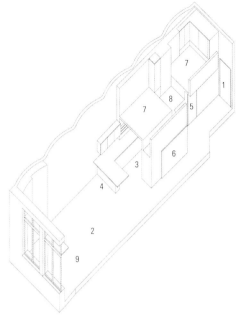

1. Entrance   6. Closet
2. Living area   7. Sleeping
3. Kitchen   platform
4. Dining area   8. Catwalk
5. Bedroom   9. Light shell

Axonometrioc view

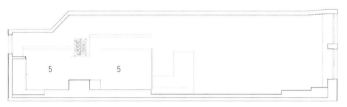

Mezzanine plan

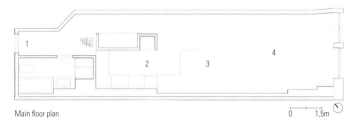

Main floor plan

0   1,5m

1. Entrance
2. Kitchen
3. Dining area
4. Living room
5. Sleeping platform

The bed platform bridges the space above
the kitchen and is open to the living area.The
staircase fits perfectly into the structure which,
on the inside, serves as a storage system.

Der Steg, wo sich das Bett befindet, ist über der
Küche, die zum Wohnzimmer hin offen ist. Die
Treppe ist nahtlos in das Gefüge integriert, im
Inneren dient sie als Stauraum.

La passerelle où se trouve le lit est au dessus
de la cuisine, ouverte sur le séjour. L'escalier
s'intègre parfaitement dans la structure qui,
au niveau de sa partie intérieure, sert de
rangements.

La pasarela donde se ubica la cama, está
encima de la cocina, abierta hacia la sala de
estar. La escalera se integra perfectamente en
la estructura que, por su parte interior, sirve de
sistema de almacenaje.

LOFT WITH
SPIRAL STAIRCASE

60 m² | 645.83 sq ft

——

MATTIA OLIVIERO BIANCHI - MOB ARCHITECTS

——

ROME, ITALY

——

© VINCENZO TAMBASCO

This historic downtown building from the 1850s has been remodeled into a refined and eccentric loft with an industrial feel. The choice was made to construct an ample, luminous space, with its two levels joined by a spectacular sinusoidal staircase that dominates the scene. The materials and the custom-made furniture help create an exclusive atmosphere overall.

Diese Wohnung liegt in einem historischen Gebäude aus dem Jahr 1850 im Stadtzentrum. Bei der Umgestaltung wird sie in diesen raffinierten und exzentrischen Loft mit Fabrik-Look verwandelt. Der Architekt entschied sich, einen großzügigen und hellen Raum auf zwei Ebenen zu schaffen, die durch eine großartige sinusförmige Treppe verbunden sind, welche die Gesamtansicht beherrscht. Die eingesetzten Materialien und die nach Maß gefertigten Möbel tragen dazu bei, dem gesamten Ensemble eine äußerst exklusive Atmosphäre zu verleihen.

Situé dans un bâtiment historique de 1850 du centre-ville, ce bien a été transformé en un loft raffiné et excentrique avec un air industriel. On a opté pour la construction d'un espace vaste et lumineux réparti sur deux niveaux unis par un escalier spectaculaire sinusoïdal qui domine toute la vue. Les matériaux utilisés, ainsi que les meubles fabriqués sur mesure contribuent à créer une atmosphère très exclusive à tout l'ensemble.

Ubicado en un edificio histórico de 1850 del centro de la ciudad, la reforma convierte esta vivienda en un refinado y excéntrico loft con aire industrial. Se opta por construir un espacio amplio y luminoso distribuido en dos niveles unidos por una espectacular escalera sinusoidal que domina toda la vista. Los materiales utilizados así como los muebles hechos a medida contribuyen a crear una atmósfera muy exclusiva a todo el conjunto.

The nearly unobstructed lower level is made up of the living room, dining room/kitchen, and the main bathroom.

Im unteren Teil der Wohnstätte finden wir, praktisch ohne Auflösung der Kontinuität, das Wohnzimmer, das Esszimmer mit Küche und das große Bad.

Au rez-de-chaussée, pratiquement sans solution de continuité, se trouvent le séjour, la cuisine-salle à manger et la principale salle de bains.

En la parte inferior de la vivienda encontramos, prácticamente sin solución de continuidad, la sala de estar, la cocina-comedor y el baño principal.

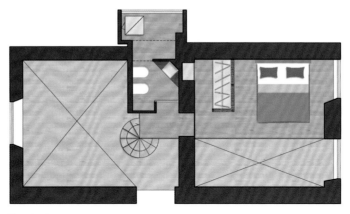

Mezzanine plan

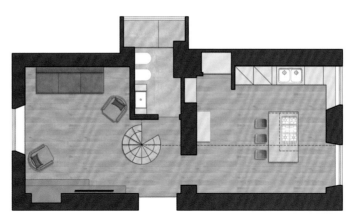

Main floor plan

Practically nothing remains of the original structure. Walls and internal partitions have been eliminated in an effort to achieve a seamless effect.

Von der Gestaltung und der ursprünglichen Struktur wurde praktisch nichts beibehalten, Innenwände und Aufteilungen im Inneren wurden beseitigt, wodurch es gelang, den Räumen eine großartige Geräumigkeit zu geben.

De la conception et structure d'origine, il ne reste pratiquement rien. Les murs et cloisons ont été retirés pour laisser place à des espaces dans une grande continuité.

Del diseño y estructura original no se respeta prácticamente nada, se han eliminando paredes y particiones internas y se ha conseguido dar una gran continuidad a los espacios.

The upper level holds the bedroom and a
second bath. The completely restored vaulted
ceiling, made of brick, helps establish continuity
between the living room and the bedroom.

Auf der oberen Ebene befinden sich
das Schlafzimmer und ein zweites Bad.
Die vollständig restaurierte Decke aus
Ziegelsteinen in Bogenform trägt dazu bei,
eine Kontinuität zwischen Wohnzimmer und
Schlafzimmer herzustellen.

Au niveau supérieur se trouvent la chambre
et une deuxième salle de bains. Le plafond,
entièrement rénové, de briques en forme de
voûte, contribue à établir une continuité entre
le salon et la chambre.

En el nivel superior se ubican la habitación
y un segundo baño. El techo, restaurado por
completo, de ladrillos en forma de bóveda,
contribuye a establecer una continuidad entre
el salón y la habitación.

BEAM HOUSE
LOFT

62 m² | 667.36 sq ft

RAUL MONTERO Y EMILIO PARDO / RUE SOLUCIONES ESPACIALES

LOGROÑO, SPAIN

© CRISTINA NÚÑEZ BAQUEDANO

Because of the limited budget for this renovation, the decision was made not to make changes to the kitchen and bathroom, but rather to focus the work on the facade and the living spaces. The new layout eliminates walls, leaving a large central space for the living and dining area; the closed spaces are grouped on one side. The beam that dominates the space is reinforced by two diagonal metal frames that are sunk into the party walls.

Aufgrund des geringen Budgets für die Renovierung, wurde beschlossen, die Nassräume, also Küche und Bad, nicht anzutasten und den Umbau auf die Fassade und die Wohn- und Schlafbereiche zu konzentrieren. Die neue Raumaufteilung beseitigt die Wände und hinterlässt einen großen zentralen Raum, der Wohnzimmer und Esszimmer beherbergt, wodurch die aufgegliederten Räume auf der gleichen Seite der Wohnung platziert werden. Der Balken, der den Raum beherrscht, wird mit zwei diagonalen Metallprofilen verstärkt, die in die Scheidemauern eingebettet sind.

Le budget des travaux est très serré, par conséquent il a été décidé de ne pas toucher les pièces humides telles que la cuisine et la salle de bains, mais plutôt de se concentrer sur la rénovation de la façade et des espaces de vie et de nuit. La nouvelle répartition prévoit le retrait des murs laissant ainsi un grand espace central qui fait place au salon et à la salle à manger, avec des espaces compartimentés sur un même côté de l'habitation. La poutre, élément essentiel de l'espace, renforce les deux profilés métalliques diagonaux encastrés dans les médianes.

Se dispone de un presupuesto reducido para acometer la reforma, con lo que se decide no actuar sobre los cuartos húmedos, cocina y cuarto de baño y centrar la reforma en la fachada y las zonas de día y de noche. La nueva distribución elimina paredes, dejando un gran espacio central que acoge las actividades de salón y comedor, situando los espacios compartimentados a un mismo lado de la vivienda. La viga que protagoniza el espacio se refuerza con dos perfiles metálicos diagonales empotrados en las medianeras.

The living/dining room features a horizontally folded panel that creates a sizeable bench to be used for seating or as a counter space, as needed.

Im Wohn-Esszimmer finden wir eine horizontal gefaltete Verkleidung, die eine große Unterlage schafft, die je nach Bedarf des Bewohners als Sitzgelegenheit oder Arbeitsfläche dienen kann.

Dans le salon-salle à manger se trouve un panneau plié à l'horizontale pour créer un grand banc qui peut aussi servir d'assise ou de plan de travail selon les besoins de l'utilisateur.

En el salón-comedor encontramos un panelado plegado en horizontal para generar una gran bancada que puede servir como asiento o encimera según las necesidades del usuario.

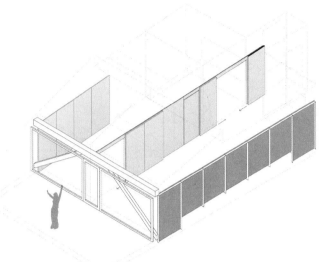

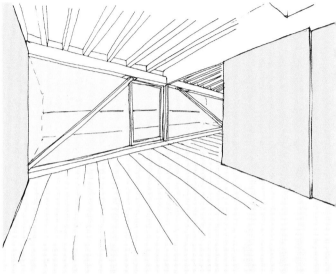

To maximize the relationship with the outdoors, the solid facade has been replaced by a large picture window; sliding panels between the rooms create a continuous and changeable space.

Um die Beziehung zur Außenseite zu maximieren, wird die vorhandene massive Fassade durch ein großes Fenster ersetzt, und Schiebeflügel zwischen den Wohnräumen angebracht, um einen durchgehenden und wandelbaren Raum zu schaffen.

Pour maximiser la relation avec l'extérieur, la façade massive existante a été remplacée par une grande baie vitrée et des vantaux coulissants entre les pièces afin de créer un espace continu et changeant.

Para maximizar la relación con el exterior se sustituye la fachada maciza existente por un gran ventanal, y se disponen paneles correderos entre las estancias para generar un espacio continuo y cambiante.

Before intervention plan

1. Entrance
2. Room 1
3. Bedroom
4. Balcony
5. Dining room
6. Bathroom
7. Kitchen
8. Storage room

After intervention plan

1. Entrance
2. Living/Dining room
3. Balcony
4. Bedroom
5. Bathroom
6. Kitchen
7. Storage room

NEW YORK-STYLE LOFT IN BARCELONA

64 m² | 688.9 sq ft

DRÖM LIVING

BARCELONA, SPAIN

© NÉSTOR MARCHADOR

The initial aims of the renovation plan were to increase the amount of natural light, and create an innovative custom design that would maintain the building's industrial essence. This was achieved by completely redistributing the spaces, eliminating unnecessary partitions, and opening up new accesses to the terrace. The overall look exudes the characteristic strength of New York lofts, with its strong personality, its clear mastery of dark tones, and the ever-present touches of wood.

Zum Zeitpunkt des Umbaus werden die vorrangigen Ziele definiert, den Einfall von Tageslicht zu steigern und eine maßgeschneiderte und innovative Gestaltung zu konzipieren, die den gewerblichen Charakter des Ortes aufrechterhält. Hierfür wurden die Räume vollständig neu aufgeteilt, nicht notwendige Trennwände entfernt und neue Zugänge zur Terrasse geöffnet. Die Gesamtgestaltung des Raumes verströmt den für New Yorker Lofts typischen Charakter, mit viel Persönlichkeit und der eindeutigen Vorherrschaft dunkler Töne und einem Hauch Holz.

Au moment des travaux, on s'est fixé comme objectif principal d'augmenter l'entrée de la lumière naturelle et concevoir une conception sur mesure et innovante qui conserve l'essence industrielle des lieux. Pour cela, on a entièrement redéfini les espaces, supprimé les cloisons inutiles et créé de nouveaux accès à la terrasse. La conception globale de l'espace marque le caractère fort, propre des lofts new-yorkais avec beaucoup de personnalité et une dominance claire des tons sombres et de la présence des touches de bois.

En el momento de la reforma se fijan como objetivos primordiales incrementar la entrada de luz natural y concebir un diseño a medida e innovador que mantenga la esencia industrial del lugar. Para ello se redistribuyen por completo los espacios, se eliminan tabiques innecesarios y se abren nuevos accesos a la terraza. El diseño global del espacio desprende el carácter fuerte, propio de los lofts neoyorquinos, con mucha personalidad y con un claro dominio de los tonos oscuros y la presencia de toques de madera.

The living room and both bedrooms have one main wall made of the original restored brick; this adds warmth to the entire dwelling.

Sowohl im Wohnzimmer als auch in den beiden Schlafzimmern wird der ursprüngliche Ziegelstein wiederverwertet und an einer der Hauptwände freigelegt, was der gesamten Wohnstätte Wärme verleiht.

On a récupéré les briques d'origine du salon et des deux chambres, apparentes sur un pan des murs principaux, ce qui confère de la chaleur à tout le loft.

Tanto en el salón como en los dos dormitorios se recupera el ladrillo original dejándolo al descubierto en una de las paredes principales, con lo que se consigue dotar de calidez toda la vivienda.

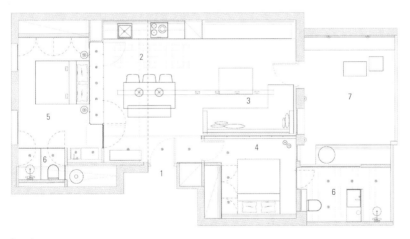

Floor plan

1. Entrance
2. Dining room/
   Kitchen
3. Living room
4. Guest Bedroom
5. Bedroom
6. Bathroom
7. Terrace

The master bedroom, located in the space once occupied by the former kitchen, is attached to a bathroom that was once accessed from the outside. A glass divider adds spaciousness to the bedroom and connects it with the rest of the home.

Der Hauptraum, der sich an der Stelle der ehemaligen Küche befindet, verbindet sich mit dem Bad, das früher von außen zugänglich war. Der Einsatz einer Glasabtrennung schenkt dem Schlafzimmer Geräumigkeit und verbindet es mit der übrigen Wohnung.

La chambre parentale, située dans l'ancienne cuisine, vient s'unir à une salle de bains, accessible initialement depuis l'extérieur. Le recours à une séparation en verre donne à la chambre une sensation d'espace et la relie au reste du loft.

La habitación principal, situada donde se encontraba la antigua cocina, se une a un baño al que inicialmente se accedía por el exterior. El uso de una separación acristalada dota el dormitorio de amplitud y lo conecta con el resto de la vivienda.

LIVING
UNDER A ROOF

64 m² | 688.89 sq ft

PRISCA PELLERIN ARCHITECTURE & INTÉRIEUR

IVRY-SUR-SEINE, FRANCE

© HUGO HÉBRARD

This penthouse was remodeled with a view to creating a bright, airy space; it was opened up by removing the inside walls to allow light to circulate. The wall colors, white gold and pale gray, were chosen according to the pathway of the sun; this is true also of the textures that are used-brick, matte and satin finish paints, polished concrete, and leather. This combination creates a light-and-shadow play that dances with dynamic lighting throughout the day. The furniture, which is built low to the ground, enhances the perspective.

Beim Umbau dieses Dachgeschosses soll ein freier und durchscheinender Raum entstehen, weshalb der Planer beschloss, die Räume zu öffnen und dadurch die Aufsplitterung rückgängig zu machen, damit das Licht zirkulieren kann. Das Weißgold und Hellgrau der Wände wurde im Einklang mit dem Verlauf Sonne ausgewählt, ebenso wie die eingesetzten Texturen (Ziegelstein, matte und satinierte Farbe, polierter Beton, Leder). Diese Kombination erzeugt ein Schattenspiel, das die dynamische Beleuchtung den ganzen Tag begleitet. Die niedrigen Möbel erhöhen die Perspektive.

Lors de la rénovation de ce dernier étage, on a cherché à créer un espace clair et ouvert. On a donc opté pour l'ouverture des espaces en le décompartimentant afin que la lumière puisse circuler. La couleur des murs, or blanc et gris clair, a été choisie selon la trajectoire du soleil, ainsi que les matériaux utilisés (briques, peinture mate et satinée, béton ciré, cuir). Cette combinaison créé un jeu d'ombres qui accompagne l'éclairage dynamique tout au long de la journée. Les meubles bas augmentent la perspective.

En la renovación de este ático se busca crear un espacio claro y diáfano, por lo que se opta por abrir los espacios, descompartimentándolo para que circule la luz. El color de las paredes, oro blanco y gris claro, se escoge acorde con la trayectoria del sol, así como las texturas utilizadas (ladrillo, pintura mate y satinada, hormigón pulido, cuero). Esta combinación crea un juego de sombras que acompaña la iluminación dinámica durante todo el día. Los muebles de baja altura aumentan la perspectiva.

The view from the bedroom to the living room is unobstructed. Light enters through the skylights, flooding the entire passageway. Across from the kitchen, behind a glass-paned door, is the bathroom.

Vom Schlafzimmer bis zum Wohnzimmer kann der Blick ohne Hindernis frei schweifen. Das Licht tritt durch die Fenster in der Decke ein und durchflutet den gesamten Verlauf des Flurs. Hinter einer Glastür befindet sich das Bad, und davor liegt die Küche.

De la chambre au séjour, la vue est entièrement dégagée sur son passage. La lumière pénètre à travers les fenêtres du toit et inonde tout le couloir. La salle de bains se trouve derrière une porte en verre en face de la cuisine.

Desde el dormitorio a la sala de estar la vista no encuentra ningún obstáculo en su camino. La luz entra por las ventanas del techo e inunda todo el recorrido el pasillo. Tras una puerta acristalada se encuentra el baño, y frente a él, la cocina.

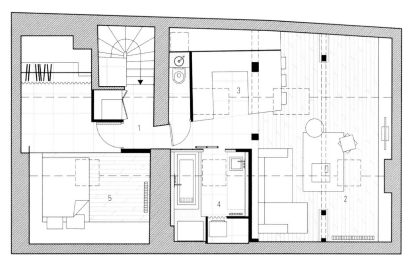

Floor plan

1. Entrance
2. Living room
3. Kitchen/Dining room
4. Bathroom
5. Bedroom

LOFT
"CAN FELIPA"

64 m² | 688.89 sq ft

JOSEP CANO

BARCELONA, SPAIN

© NICOLÁS FOTOGRAFÍA

This old urban industrial space was carefully renovated into a home where height is a key factor. The fact that original elements were restored converts the space into the very essence of a loft. This essence is extended as new structures and materials are added that provide luminosity while maintaining a uniform color scheme. The layout meets all the requirements of comfortable living within a serene, welcoming environment.

Bei dieser Wohnung, die in einem alten Gewerberaum der Stadt liegt, wird ein behutsamer Eingriff durchgeführt, bei dem die Deckenhöhe die Hauptfigur ist. Die Renovierung der Originalelemente schenkt dem Raum die wahre Essenz eines Lofts. Dieses Gefühl wird verstärkt durch die Einbindung von Strukturen und neuer Materialien, die ihm Helle geben, wobei eine farbliche Gleichförmigkeit erhalten bleibt. Die Räume sind so aufgeteilt, dass Sie alle Bedürfnisse erfüllen, um in einer ruhigen und einladenden Atmosphäre komfortabel leben zu können.

Dans ce logement, situé dans un ancien hangar industriel de la ville, ont été réalisés de minutieux travaux mettant en avant la hauteur. La restauration des éléments d'origine apporte l'essence du loft à l'espace. Cette sensation s'amplifie avec l'intégration des structures et des nouveaux matériaux qui lui confèrent de la luminosité tout en conservant une uniformité chromatique. Les espaces sont répartis selon les besoins afin de pouvoir vivre aisément dans un cadre serein et accueillant.

En esta vivienda, situada en un antiguo espacio industrial de la ciudad, se lleva a cabo una intervención cuidadosa donde la altura es la protagonista. La restauración de los elementos originales aporta la esencia loft al espacio. Esta sensación se magnifica con la incorporación de estructuras y nuevos materiales que le dan luminosidad manteniendo una uniformidad cromática. Los espacios están distribuidos cubriendo las necesidades para poder vivir confortablemente dentro de un ambiente sereno y acogedor.

The height of the roof, so crucial to the historic industrial use of the loft, made it possible to install a mezzanine, which is the site for perfectly differentiated zones for work and rest.

Man nutzt die für die ehemalige gewerbliche Nutzung des Lofts typische Deckenhöhe, um ein Zwischengeschoss zu errichten, wo sich - perfekt voneinander abgetrennt - die Arbeits- und Ruhebereiche befinden.

On a profité de la hauteur sous plafond de l'ancien usage industriel du loft afin de créer une mezzanine sur laquelle sont parfaitement distincts les espaces de travail et de détente.

Se aprovecha la altura de techo propia del antiguo uso industrial del loft para levantar un altillo en el que se ubican, perfectamente diferenciadas, las zonas de trabajo y de descanso.

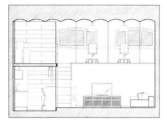
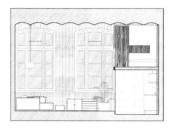

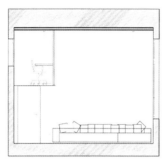

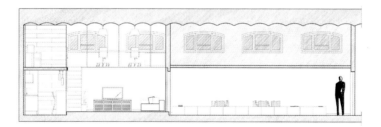

Sections

The plans and the sections clearly show how the elevated platform has been the key to making the best possible use of the space, with a bright and spacious area on the ground floor for daytime use.

Sowohl bei den Grundrissen als in den Anschnittprofilen lässt sich erkennen, wie mithilfe der errichteten Plattform der Raum optimal ausgenutzt werden konnte, wodurch ein großzügiger und durchscheinender Wohnbereich auf der unteren Ebene entsteht.

Grâce à la plateforme surélevée, il est possible d'apprécier aussi bien dans les étages que dans les parties, la maximisation de l'espace en laissant un espace de vie, vaste et ouvert, au rez-de-chaussée.

Tanto en las plantas como en las secciones se puede apreciar como mediante la plataforma elevada se ha conseguido sacar el máximo provecho al espacio, dejando una zona de día amplia y diáfana en la planta inferior.

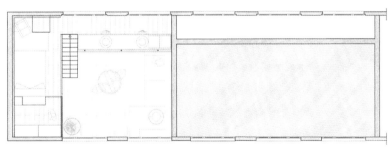

Mezzanine plan

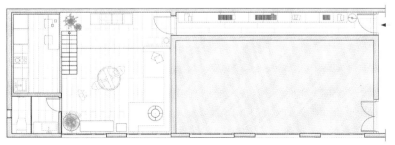

Ground floor plan

RUSTIC-STYLE LOFT

65 m² | 699.6 sq ft

—

DE GOMA / NEUS CASANOVA

—

BARCELONA, SPAIN

—

© NEUS CASANOVA

Here, the entire original structure was revamped to increase its functionality and spaciousness, and provide a higher quality of life. The living area is a large open space shared by the living and dining rooms; the highlights here are the original rock walls and the timber roof beams. Some of the borders of the original hydraulic floor tiles have been preserved; these delineate different distribution areas, such as the foyer/study and the dining room; these maintain the footprint of the previous apartment.

Die ursprüngliche Struktur wird umfassend renoviert, um deren Funktionalität zu verbessern, das Gefühl von Geräumigkeit zu steigern und Lebensqualität zu gewinnen. Der Wohnbereich ist ein großer offener Raum, den sich Wohnzimmer und Esszimmer teilen, besonders erwähnenswert sind hier eine Originalsteinwand und die Deckenbalken aus Holz. Einige Randverzierungen aus Zementfliesen bleiben erhalten, wodurch sich die Verteilerbereiche wie Eingangsbereich-Arbeitszimmer und Esszimmer abgrenzen lassen, und die Spuren der vorherigen Wohnung erhalten bleiben.

La structure d'origine a été entièrement rénovée afin d'améliorer sa fonctionnalité, augmenter la sensation de grandeur et gagner en qualité de vie. L'espace de vie est un grand espace ouvert que partagent le salon et la salle à manger où l'on distingue la présence du mur de pierre d'origine et les poutres en bois du plafond. Certaines frises du carrelage hydraulique d'origine permettent de délimiter les espaces tels que l'entrée-bureau et la salle à manger tout en conservant l'empreinte de l'ancien appartement.

Se reforma de manera integral la estructura original para mejorar su funcionalidad, aumentar la sensación de amplitud y ganar calidad de vida. La zona de día es un gran espacio abierto que comparten salón y comedor, en el que destaca la presencia de la pared de piedra original, y las vigas de madera del techo. Se mantienen algunas cenefas de las baldosas hidráulicas originales que permiten delimitar zonas de distribución, como el recibidor-estudio y el comedor, y conservan la huella del piso anterior.

The combination of white walls, exposed brick, and wood give this cottage-style space a warm and homey feel.

Die Kombination von weißen Wänden, sichtbaren Backsteinen und Holz verleihen dem Raum eine rustikale und zugleich warme Atmosphäre.

La combinaison des murs blancs, de la brique apparente et du bois confère à l'espace un côté à la fois rustique et chaleureux.

La combinación de paredes blancas, ladrillo visto y madera confieren al espacio un punto rústico y cálido a la vez.

At night, the welcoming foyer/study serves as an open space that lets natural light into the bedroom.

Der Eingangsbereich mit Arbeitszimmer heißt den Besucher in dieser Wohnung willkommen, er fungiert als durchscheinender Raum im Schlafbereich und ermöglicht den Einfall von Tageslicht in das Schlafzimmer.

L'entrée-bureau souhaite la bienvenue à la maison et joue le rôle d'un espace ouvert dans la partie nuit permettant ainsi à la lumière naturelle d'entrer dans la chambre.

El recibidor-estudio da la bienvenida a la casa y actúa como un espacio diáfano en la zona de noche, permitiendo la entrada de luz natural al dormitorio.

The bunk that comprises the sleeping quarters makes the most of the limited space; its headboard is the outer wall of a closet, and there are two large drawers beneath it.

Das Schlafzimmer mit seinen sehr kleinen Abmessungen wurde so konzipiert, um den Raum durch einen Wandschrank am Kopfteil und zwei große Fächer im unteren Teil maximal auszunutzen.

La chambre très exiguë a été conçue de sorte à profiter au maximum de l'espace avec une armoire comme tête de lit et deux grands caissons au pied.

El dormitorio, de dimensiones muy pequeñas, fue diseñado para aprovechar al máximo el espacio con un armario en su cabezal y dos grandes cajones en su parte inferior.

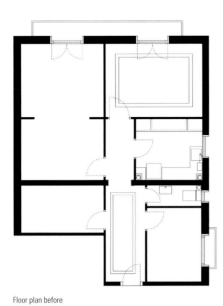

Floor plan before

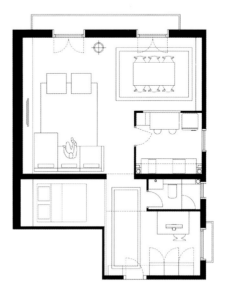

Floor plan after

STYLISH COSY LOFT

69.67 m² | 750 sq ft

—

LEONIDAS TRAMPOUKIS, ELENI PETALOTI / LOT OFFICE FOR ARCHITECTURE

—

NEW YORK, NEW YORK, UNITED STATES

—

© LOT

This loft is set in a historic fireworks factory in the heart of one of the liveliest neighborhoods in Brooklyn. It features refurbished wooden flooring, hand-made furniture, white walls, and exposed ductwork. When this dwelling was being planned, every effort was made to provide a balance between energy efficiency and flexible space. The wall between the day zone and private areas was removed and replaced by a curtain; this also allows it to be turned into an intimate space for guests.

Dieser Loft wird in einer historischen Fabrik für Feuerwerkskörper im Herzen einer der dynamischsten Bezirke von Brooklyn errichtet. Der Boden aus wiederverwertetem Holz wird mit maßgefertigtem Mobiliar, weißen Wänden und offen verlegten Rohrleitungen kombiniert. Bei der Planung dieser Wohnstätte wurde versucht, jederzeit ein Gleichgewicht zwischen der Energieeffizienz und dem flexiblen Raum aufrechtzuerhalten. Die Wand zwischen dem Aufenthaltsbereich und privaten Bereich wurde entfernt und durch einen Vorhang ersetzt, mit dessen Hilfe er sich auch in einen privaten Bereich für Gäste verwandeln lässt.

Ce loft a été construit dans une usine historique de fusées au cœur d'un des quartiers les plus dynamiques de Brooklyn. Le sol en bois réutilisé se combine avec le mobilier fait sur mesure, les murs blancs et les conduites apparentes. Cela procure à tout moment un équilibre entre l'efficacité énergétique et l'espace flexible au moment de planifier cette habitation. Le mur entre l'espace de vie et la partie nuit a été retiré pour utiliser à la place un rideau qui permet aussi de la transformer en un espace intime pour invités.

Este loft se erige en una histórica fábrica de cohetes en el corazón de uno de los barrios más dinámicos de Brooklyn. Se combina el suelo de madera reutilizada, con mobiliario hecho a medida, paredes blancas y tuberías al descubierto. En todo momento se procura mantener un equilibrio entre la eficiencia energética y el espacio flexible a la hora de planear esta vivienda. Se elimina la pared entre el área de día y el espacio privado, utilizando una cortina en sustitución, que también permite convertirlo en un espacio íntimo para invitados.

The kitchen island is made of crates that were used to ship photographs to an exhibition. Beside hangs a large blackboard that contrasts with the pale tones that so decidedly prevail elsewhere.

Die Kücheninsel wurde aus Versandkisten für die Fotos einer Ausstellung gefertigt. Daneben finden wir eine große schwarze Schiefertafel, die mit den hellen Tönen kontrastiert, die in der übrigen Wohnstätte absolut vorherrschen.

L'îlot de la cuisine a été créé à partir de caisses d'expédition de photographies pour une exposition. À proximité se trouve un grand tableau noir qui contraste avec les tons clairs prédominant de manière absolue le reste de l'habitation.

La isla de la cocina se crea a partir de cajas de envío de fotografías para una exposición. A su lado encontramos una gran pizarra negra que contrasta con los tonos claros que predomina de forma absoluta an en el resto de la vivienda.

The completely white bedroom, with its views of the street, is the perfect retreat for an end-of-day rest.

Das komplett weiße Schlafzimmer mit Blick auf die Straße ist der perfekte Rückzugsort, um sich am Ende des Tages auszuruhen.

La chambre entièrement blanche avec vue sur la rue est la retraite parfaite pour se reposer en fin de journée.

La habitación completamente blanca y con vistas a la calle, es el retiro perfecto para descansar al final del día.

FROM SHOP TO LOFT

70 m² | 753.5 sq ft

R3ARCHITETTI

TURIN, ITALY

© JACOPO GALLITTO (TWINPIXEL)

Loft duplex constructed over an old store for a young businessman. The tall narrow look of the dwelling is used to embody an architectural section design, invoking a loft that turns into a duplex. The layout places the living and working zones, along with the kitchen and master bedroom, on the lower floor. On the second level there is a bedroom and another study/work space that overlooks the living room.

Maisonette-Loft, der für einen jungen Unternehmer über einem ehemaligen Geschäft erbaut wurde. Hier werden die Höhe und Enge der Wohnstätte eingesetzt, um ein architektonisches Design in Trakten zu beleben, indem ein Loft konzipiert wird, das einer Maisonette-Wohnung Leben einhaucht. Die Raumaufteilung ist so entworfen, dass Wohn- und Arbeitsbereich, Küche und Hauptschlafzimmer in der unteren Etage liegen. Auf der zweiten Ebene befinden sich ein Schlafzimmer und ein weiterer Studier- und Arbeitsbereich mit Blick auf das Wohnzimmer.

Loft duplex construit au-dessus d'un ancien magasin pour jeune entrepreneur. La hauteur et l'étroitesse du loft sont utilisées pour donner vie à une conception architectonique en section imaginant un loft qui donne vie à un duplex. La répartition est prévue de sorte que l'espace de vie et de travail, avec la cuisine et la chambre parentale soient à l'étage inférieur. Au premier étage se trouvent la chambre et un autre bureau/ espace de travail avec vue sur le séjour.

Loft dúplex construido encima de una antigua tienda para un joven empresario. La altura y estrechez de la vivienda se utilizan para dar vida a un diseño arquitectónico en sección, imaginando un loft que da vida a un dúplex. La distribución está contemplada de forma que la zona de vivir y trabajar, junto con la cocina y la habitación principal están en la planta inferior. En el segundo nivel encontramos la habitación y otra área de estudio/trabajo con vistas a la sala de estar.

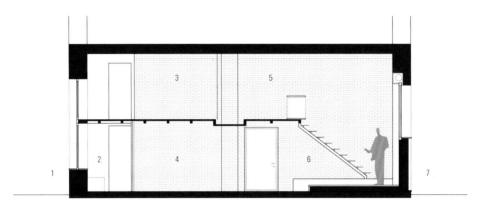

Longitudinal section

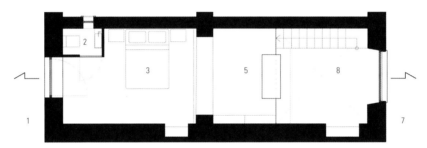

Second floor plan

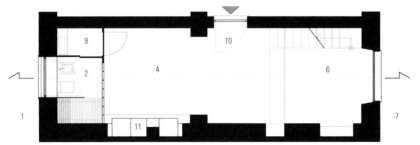

Ground floor plan

1. Courtyard
2. Bathroom
3. Bedroom
4. Dining room/Working space
5. Studying room/Working space
6. Living room/Meeting room
7. Street side
8. Empty space over the living room
9. Dressing room
10. Entrance
11. Kitchen

To increase the sense of spaciousness, the walls have been painted white, and two large windows have been installed in the side walls to allow natural light to enter.

Um das Gefühl von Geräumigkeit zu steigern, wurden die Wände weiß gestrichen, und an den Seitenwänden der Wohnung wurden zwei große Fenster herausgebrochen, damit das Tageslicht einfallen kann.

Pour augmenter la sensation d'espace, les murs ont été peints en blanc et les deux grandes fenêtres ont été ouvertes sur les murs latéraux de l'appartement afin de laisser entrer la lumière naturelle.

Para aumentar la sensación de amplitud, las paredes han sido pintadas en color blanco y se han abierto dos grandes ventanas en las paredes laterales del apartamento para que pueda entrar la luz natural.

In this multi-functional loft, the areas that are not used for working, like the kitchen and bedroom, are hidden by curtains; this allows inhabitants to move quickly from one space to another.

In diesem multifunktional ausgelegten Loft sind die Bereiche, die nicht zum Arbeiten gedacht sind, wie Küche oder Schlafzimmer, hinter Vorhängen verborgen, die einen schnellen Übergang von einem Wohnraum zum anderen ermöglichen.

Dans ce loft conçu de manière multifonctionnelle, les parties non destinées au travail telles que la cuisine ou la chambre sont dissimulées derrière des rideaux et permettent une rapide transition d'un espace à l'autre.

En este loft diseñado de manera multifuncional, las áreas no destinadas a trabajar, como la cocina o la habitación, queden escondidas por cortinas que permiten una rápida transición de un espacio al otro.

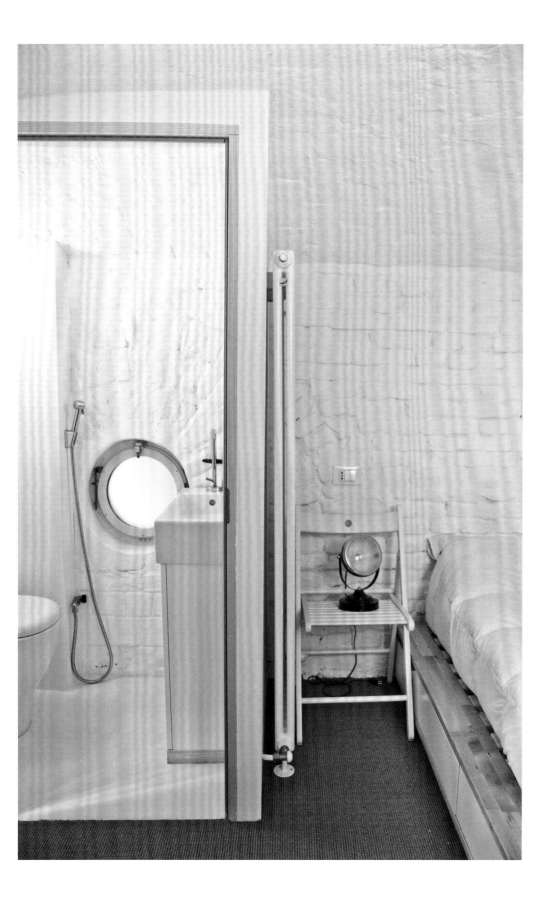

BOOKBOX
LOFT

70 m² | 753.20 sq ft

—

MODEL:NA ARCHITEKCI

—

POZNÁN, POLAND

—

© MARCIN RATAJCZAK

With a view to creating a home that is completely aligned with the owners' person-alities and needs, the entire space has been divided into four clearly defined zones; these can be part of one open space, but can also assert their independence from each other. This is achieved by separating the living spaces with sliding doors. This allows the two owners to get along easily and respect each other's needs; but it leaves the essence of the loft intact.

Um eine Wohnstätte zu schaffen, die sich ganz an die Persönlichkeit und die Anfor-derungen der Eigentümer anpasst, wird der Gesamtraum in vier deutlich definierte Bereiche aufgeteilt, die einen durchscheinenden Gemeinschaftsbereich bilden, doch wiederum ihre Unabhängigkeit bewahren können. Hierfür werden die Bereiche des jeweiligen Wohnbereichs mittels Schiebetüren getrennt. So können beide Eigentümer gleichzeitig dort wohnen, während die Bedürfnisse beider respektiert werden, ohne die Essenz des Lofts einzubüßen.

Pour créer un loft qui s'adapte complètement à la personnalité et aux besoins des pro-priétaires, l'espace a été divisé en quatre parties très bien définies qui forment ainsi un espace commun ouvert tout en conservant leur indépendance. Ceci a été obtenu en séparant les espaces de chaque pièce de vie par des portes coulissantes. Ainsi, les deux propriétaires peuvent parfaitement cohabiter tout en respectant les besoins de chacun sans perdre l'essence du loft.

Con el fin de crear una vivienda que se adapte por completo a la personalidad y ne-cesidades de los propietarios, se divide el espacio total en cuatro zonas muy bien definidas, que formen un espacio común diáfano pero que a su vez puedan mantener su independencia. La forma de conseguirlo es separando las áreas de cada zona vital mediante puertas correderas. Así, los dos propietarios puede convivir perfectamente respetando las necesidades de cada uno sin perder la esencia de loft.

Floor plan

1. Hall
2. Reading room
3. Kitchen
4. Living room
5. Wardrobe
6. Bedroom
7. Bathroom

Sliding doors are open, which enables
free movement of air, sound and people

The creation of zones and private
spaces can be achieved by closing
sliding doors

When sliding doors are closed five air/
sound/people proof zones are created

One can move from one space to the other through the sliding doors; making the space more flexible and giving each room acoustical privacy.

Durch Schiebetüren gelangt der Bewohner von einem Raum zum anderen, was den Raum flexibler macht und jedem Bereich akustisch eine Privatsphäre gibt.

Les portes coulissantes permettent de passer d'un espace à l'autre en créant un espace plus flexible et offrant de l'intimité acoustique à chaque partie.

A través de puertas correderas, se pasa de un espacio a otro haciendo el espacio más flexible y dando privacidad acústica a cada zona.

In the center there is a kitchen/dining room and a mysterious black crate that contains a closet, bookshelf, and desk.

Der zentrale Bereich umfasst Küche und Esszimmer sowie einen geheimnisvollen schwarzen Kasten, der einen Schrank, ein Bücherregal und einen Schreibtisch beherbergt.

L'espace central comprend la cuisine avec salle à manger et une mystérieuse caisse noire qui renferme une armoire, une bibliothèque et un bureau.

La zona central incluye la cocina con el comedor y una misteriosa caja negra, que integra un armario, una librería y un escritorio.

The other three sections of the dwelling are the living room, the dressing room, and the night zone; that is, the bedroom and the bathroom.

Die anderen drei Bereiche der Wohnstätte sind Wohnzimmer, Ankleidezimmer und Schlafbereich mit Bad und Schlafzimmer.

Les trois autres espaces du loft sont le séjour, le dressing et l'espace nuit avec la salle de bain et la chambre.

Las otras tres áreas de la vivienda son la sala de estar, el vestidor y la zona de noche con el baño y la habitación.

LOFT IN AN OLD FISHERMAN'S HOUSE

73 m² | 785.77 sq ft

—

AMBAU, TALLER D'ARQUITECTES

—

VALÈNCIA, SPAIN

—

© GERMÁN CABO

This older home is located very near a popular beach in Malvarrosa, Spain. The reinterpretation of its interior retains only those elements that actually add value, eliminating those that do not. This home now occupies the upper floor of the original building, which at one time was reached via a narrow stairway. A small platform has been added, and it appears to float in the above-kitchen space that separates the two stories.

Dieses alte Haus in der Nähe des beliebten Strandes Malvarrosa wurde bei der Renovierung seiner Innenräume neu interpretiert. Bewahrt wurden nur die Elemente, die einen Wert beisteuern, und diejenigen entfernt, die keinen Nutzen mehr hatten. Die Wohnstätte belegt jetzt die obere Etage des Originalgebäudes, das über eine schmale Treppe zu erreichen war. Eine kleine Plattform wird hinzugefügt, die mitten im Raum direkt über der Küche zu schweben scheint und den unteren Teil vom oberen trennt.

Cette ancienne maison, située à proximité de la célèbre plage de la Malvarrosa, est repensée lors des travaux de rénovation de son intérieur afin de conserver uniquement les éléments qui apportent une valeur et retirer ceux qui n'en fournissaient pas. L'habitat occupe désormais l'étage supérieur du bâtiment d'origine accessible par un escalier étroit. Une petite plateforme a été ajoutée. Elle semble flotter dans l'espace juste au dessus de la cuisine et sépare la partie inférieure de celle supérieure.

Esta antigua casa, ubicada muy cerca de la popular playa de la Malvarrosa, es reinterpretada en la reforma de sus interiores para conservar sólo aquellos elementos que aportan un valor y eliminar aquellos que no lo hacían. La vivienda ocupa ahora la planta superior de la edificación original, a la que se accedía a través de una estrecha escalera. Se añade una pequeña plataforma que parece flotar en medio del espacio justo encima de la cocina y que separa la parte inferior de la superior.

Because the owner required only one bedroom and a terrace, the plan is open, with the only partitioned room being the bathroom.

Da der Eigentümer nur einen Raum und eine Terrasse benötigt, wird der Raum als Loft ohne Teilung konzipiert, in dem nur das Bad abgetrennt ist.

Comme le propriétaire nécessite qu'une seule chambre et une terrasse, l'espace se présente comme un loft sans cloisons où seule la salle de bains est une pièce à part.

Debido a que el propietario solo necesita una habitación y una terraza, el espacio se plantea como un loft sin particiones, donde solo se aísla el baño.

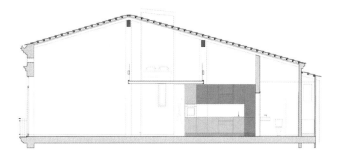

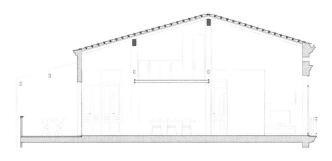

Sections

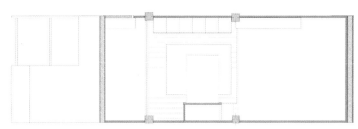

Upper floor plan

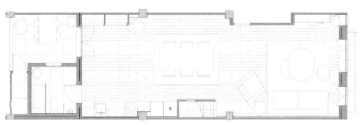

Lower floor plan

Some of the original elements of the interior design have been restored and upgraded, and then recombined with others with more modern lines.

Durch Renovieren und Kombinieren mit anderen moderneren Elementen wurden die ursprünglichen Elemente der Innengestaltung hervorgehoben.

Des éléments d'origine ont été ajoutés au design intérieur en les restaurant et en les combinant avec d'autres plus modernes.

Se han potenciado elementos originales en el diseño interior, restaurándolos y combinándolos con otros de líneas más modernas.

LOFT
"EL CAPRICHO"

75 m² | 807 sq ft

—

JOSEP CANO

—

BARCELONA, SPAIN

—

© NICOLÁS FOTOGRAFÍA

This loft is imbued with the industrial style of the original space. All the existing original fixtures, structures, and elements have been restored and designed into this interior, which was once a workshop.In a balance between old and new, these harmoniously integrated elements are reimagined as contemporary sculptures.The natural light enters through the windows into this one space in which black steel meets natural wood, leather, and weavings.

Dieser Loft ist vom Industriestil des ursprünglichen Raumes erfüllt. Alle vorhandenen Installationen, Strukturen und Originalelemente werden zurückgewonnen, um schließlich Teil der Inneneinrichtung dieser ehemaligen Werkstatt zu werden. In einer Entwicklung zwischen Alt und Neu werden die Elemente in perfekter Harmonie eingebunden und als zeitgenössische Skulpturen behandelt. Der Zugang zu Tageslicht wird durch Fenster im gleichen Raum verstärkt, in dem schwarzer Stahl mit natürlichem Holz, Leder und verschiedenen Geweben verschmilzt.

Ce loft est imprégné du style industriel de l'espace d'origine. Toutes les installations existantes ont été conservées, ainsi que les structures et les éléments d'origine pour les inclure dans la conception intérieure de cet ancien atelier. Dans une évolution entre l'ancien et le moderne, les éléments s'intègrent en parfaite harmonie et sont traités comme des sculptures contemporaines. On a favorisé l'entrée de la lumière naturelle grâce à des fenêtres dans un même espace dans lequel fusionnent l'acier noir et le bois naturel, le cuir et les tissus.

Este loft está impregnado del estilo industrial del espacio original. Se recuperan todas las instalaciones existentes, estructuras y elementos originales para pasar a formar parte del diseño interior de este antiguo taller. En una evolución entre lo viejo y lo nuevo, los elementos se incorporan en perfecta armonía y son tratados como esculturas contemporáneas. Se potencia el acceso a la luz natural a través de ventanas en un mismo espacio en el que se fusiona el acero negro con la madera natural, el cuero y los tejidos.

The decision was made to invoke the industrial history of the space and expose the ductwork and beams; in addition, materials that are clearly industrial, such as steel, are used for functional furniture; for example, the dining room table.

Der Planer beschloss, das industrielle Ambiente der Wohnstätte für sich zu beanspruchen, indem Rohrleitungen und Balken sichtbar bleiben und eindeutig industriell geprägtes Material wie Stahl bei den Funktionsmöbeln einzubinden, wie etwa hier beim Esszimmertisch.

Il a été décidé de revendiquer l'air industriel du loft en laissant les canalisations et les poutres apparentes avec l'intégration de matériaux clairement industriels tels que l'acier utilisé pour des meubles fonctionnels comme la table de salle à manger.

Se decide reivindicar el aire industrial de la vivienda dejando cañerías y vigas al descubierto, e incorporando materiales claramente industriales como el acero a muebles funcionales, como la mesa del comedor.

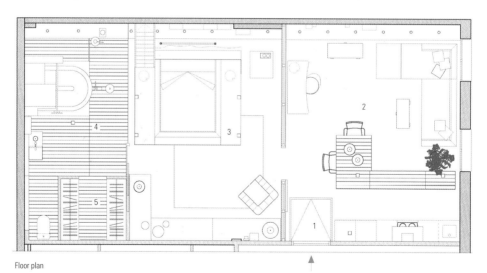

Floor plan

1. Entrance
2. Living/Dining room/
   Kitchen
3. Bedroom
4. Bathroom
5. Dressing room

In an effort to define its space, the bedroom is raised a little above floor level and set on a dark wooden platform; for privacy, it is surrounded by curtains.

Das Schlafzimmer ist durch eine Plattform aus dunklem Holz etwas vom Boden erhöht, um den Raum hervorzuheben, und von Vorhängen umgeben, um die Privatsphäre zu wahren.

La chambre est légèrement surélevée afin de mettre en relief l'espace, avec un parquet en bois sombre, entouré de rideaux pour conserver le côté intime.

El dormitorio se encuentra elevado ligeramente del suelo, para destacar el espacio, por una tarima de madera oscura, y está rodeado de cortinas para mantener la privacidad.

There is antique machinery everywhere, even in the bathroom, which is separated from the bedroom by a glass panel that allows everything inside it to be seen.

Selbst im Bad finden sich Industriemaschinen. Eine große Glastür trennt das Bad vom Schlafzimmer und lässt alle Elemente im Inneren erahnen.

On trouve de la machinerie industrielle jusque dans la salle de bains, séparée de la chambre par une grande baie vitrée qui permet d'entrevoir tous les éléments à l'intérieur.

Encontramos maquinaria industrial hasta en el baño, separado de la habitación por una gran cristalera que permite entrever todos los elementos de su interior.

RUSTIC
WHITE LOFT

80 m² | 861.11 sq ft

—

LOFT FACTORY

—

WARSAW, POLAND

—

© PIOTR GESICKI

The owners of this loft space wanted a contemporary look, but also sought chill-free warmth and comfort. The result is a simple modern home, welcoming and gentle. In this renovation, the previous kitchen and dining space are reversed. Walls and partitions are removed to achieve a clear, open space. A glass wall divides the living space into two areas: the living room with the open kitchen, and the sleeping quarters.

Die Eigentümer dieses Lofts wünschten sich einen Raum in einem modernen Look, der heimelig und behaglich jedoch nicht kalt wirken soll. Das Ergebnis ist eine modernde und einfache Wohnstätte, die gleichzeitig einladend und weich ist. Bei der Renovierung werden die Bereiche von Küche und Esszimmer in Bezug auf die ursprüngliche Gliederung gegeneinander ausgetauscht. Wände und Trennwände werden beseitigt, wodurch ein offener und durchscheinender Raum entsteht. Eine Glaswand teilt den Wohnraum in zwei Bereiche: das Wohnzimmer mit der offenen Küche und den Sitzbereich.

Les propriétaires de ce loft souhaitaient un espace au style contemporain, à la fois chaleureux et confortable, sans être froid. Le résultat est un bien moderne et simple tout en étant accueillant et doux. Lors des travaux de rénovation, les espaces de la cuisine et de la salle à manger ont été déplacés par rapport à la disposition initiale. Les murs et cloisons ont été retirés faisant place à un espace ouvert. Un mur en verre divise l'espace de vie en deux parties : le séjour avec la cuisine ouverte et l'espace détente.

Los propietarios de este loft querían un espacio de aspecto contemporáneo, pero también cálido y confortable, que no fuera frío. El resultado es una vivienda moderna y simple, a la vez que acogedora y suave. En la restauración se intercambian los espacios de la cocina y el comedor respecto a la estructura original. Se eliminan paredes y tabiques logrando un espacio abierto y diáfano. Una pared de cristal divide el espacio vital en dos áreas: la sala de estar con la cocina abierta, y la zona de descanso.

The glass wall lets in the natural light and brings the two spaces together. The brick walls and the mosaic parquet flooring add a homey touch.

Die Glaswand ermöglicht den Durchfluss von Tageslicht und vereint beide Räume. Die Kombination aus Backsteinwand und Parkettmosaik im Boden verleihen der Wohnstätte einen heimeligen Touch.

Le mur en verre laisse pénétrer la lumière naturelle et réunit les deux espaces. La combinaison brique-mur et parquet-mosaïque au sol donne une touche familiale au bien.

La pared de cristal permite el paso de la luz natural y une ambos espacios. La combinación de ladrillo-pared y parquet-mosaico en el suelo, confieren el toque hogareño de la vivienda.

The private area consists of the bedroom, with curtained shelving acting as a clothes closet, and the bathroom.

Der Privatbereich besteht aus einem Zimmer und den mit einem Vorhang bedeckten Regalen, die als Schrank fungieren, sowie einem Bad.

L'espace privatif comprend une chambre, avec des étagères recouvertes d'un rideau qui servent en même temps d'armoire, et la salle de bains.

En la zona privada está compuesta por la habitación, con estanterías cubiertas con una cortina que hacen las veces de armario, y el baño.

KABINNET LOFT

83 m² | 893.40 sq ft

——

DOUNIA HAMDOUCH, LINA LAGERSTROM / SEPTEMBRE

——

PARIS, FRANCE

——

© MARIS MEZULIS

This three-person loft was once a workshop for artisans. The clients wanted an open space with no visible appliances, and they also sought storage capacity. The decision was made to create the spaces using wood, but in a number of different forms, adapted to meet the various requirements. A glass divider separates the bedrooms from the living/dining/kitchen area, so the entire main space is large, light and airy.

Umstrukturierung eines ehemaligen Kunsthandwerkerateliers in ein Loft für drei Personen. Zu den Wünschen des Kunden zählte u. a., einen offenen Raum mit Staumöglichkeiten zu schaffen und dass die Installationen nicht sichtbar sein sollten. Der Planer entschied sich für den Einsatz von Räumen aus Holz in verschiedenen Formen, die sich an den jeweiligen Bedarf anpassen. Der Hauptraum wird durch eine Glaswand geteilt, der die Schlafzimmer vom Wohn-Esszimmer abtrennt, das die Küche einbindet, wodurch ein geräumiger, heller und durchscheinender Bereich geschaffen wird.

Transformation d'un ancien atelier d'artisans en un loft pour trois personnes. Une des demandes du client est d'avoir un espace ouvert avec des rangements et que les pièces soient dissimulées. On a opté pour l'utilisation d'espaces en bois, de différentes formes qui s'adapteront à chaque besoin. L'espace de vie est divisé par une baie vitrée qui sépare les chambres du séjour-salle à manger qui intègre la cuisine, créant ainsi un vaste espace lumineux et ouvert.

Reconversión de un antiguo taller de artesanos en un loft para tres personas. Una de las demandas del cliente es que querían un espacio abierto, con capacidad de almacenamiento y que las instalaciones no fueran visibles. Se opta por el uso de espacios de madera, de diferentes formas que se adaptaran a cada necesidad. El espacio principal está dividido por un cristal que separa las habitaciones de la sala de estar-comedor, que integra la cocina, creando una amplia zona iluminada y diáfana.

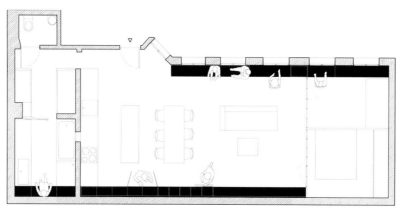

Floor plan

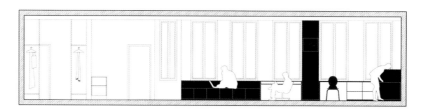

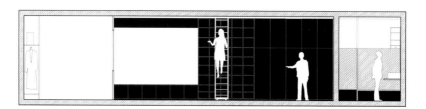

Sections

For maximum impact, the bathroom walls are clad in square white tiles, with gray trim. A large wooden bench-type cabinet hides the washing machine and holds built-in hand basins and a baby changing table.

Um optisch zu überzeugen, wurden im Bad quadratische weiße Fliesen mit grauen Holzarbeiten kombiniert. Eine große Holzbank verbirgt die Waschmaschine und bindet Waschbecken und Wickeltisch ein.

Dans la salle de bains se mélangent la faïence blanche carrée et la boiserie de couleur grise cherchant à créer un grand contraste. Un grand plan en bois sur lequel reposent deux lavabos et une table à langer pour bébés, cache la machine à laver.

En el baño se combinan el azulejo blanco cuadrado con carpintería gris, buscando causar un gran impacto. Un banco de madera grande esconde la lavadora, e integra los lavamanos y un cambiador para niños.

SCANDINAVIAN LOFT

85 m² | 914.93 sq ft

———

INDRĖ SUNKLODIENĖ / INARCH - INTERJERO ARCHITEKHTURA

———

VANCOUVER, BRITISH COLUMBIA, CANADA

———

© LEONAS GARBAČAUSKAS

This loft, with its decidedly Scandinavian look, was designed to be lived in by a young couple. The kitchen, dining room, and living room are located on the lower of its two floors. The combinations of the materials on its walls, floors, and furniture—wood, cement, concrete, and tiling—contribute both contrast and warmth to the space. Every inch is made use of; for example, the staircase is used for storage, and a bench is built over the radiator.

Dieser Loft mit eindeutig skandinavischem Look wurde für ein junges Paar konzipiert. In zwei Etagen gegliedert, befinden sich auf der unteren Etage Küche, Esszimmer und Wohnzimmer. Die Kombination von Materialien an Wänden, Böden und Möbeln wie beispielsweise Holz, Zement, Beton und Fliesen geben dem Raum gleichsam Kontrast und Wärme. Alle Ecken werden maximal ausgenutzt, folglich wird die Treppe als Stauraum genutzt und auf dem Heizkörper wird eine Bank angebracht.

Ce loft au look clairement scandinave est conçu pour être habité pour un couple de jeunes. Organisé sur deux niveaux, le r ez-de-chaussée comprend la cuisine, la salle à manger et le séjour. La combinaison de matériaux sur les murs, sols et meubles tels que le bois, le ciment, le béton et la faïence apporte du contraste tout en donnant de la chaleur à l'espace. Tous les recoins ont été maximisés, ainsi l'escalier sert d'espace de rangement avec un banc au-dessus du radiateur.

Este loft de look claramente escandinavo, está concebido para ser habitado por una pareja joven. Organizado en dos plantas, en la zona inferior encontramos la cocina, el comedor y sala de estar. La combinación de materiales en paredes, suelos y muebles como la madera, cemento, hormigón y azulejos aportan contraste a la par que calidez al espacio. Se aprovechan al máximo todos los rincones, así la escalera se usa como espacio de almacenamiento y se construye un banco encima del radiador.

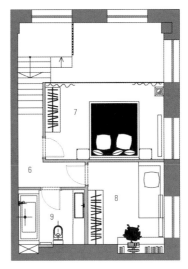

Upper floor plan

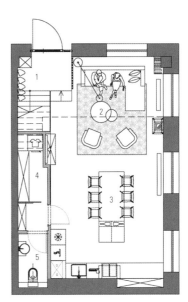

Lower floor plan

1. Entrance
2. Living room
3. Dining room
4. Storehouse
5. Toilet
6. Entrance to
   upper floor
7. Bedroom
8. Office
9. Bathroom

The bedroom on the upper floor has one wall made of glass; when the curtain is pulled back, the light can enter freely.

Eine große Scheibe trennt das Schlafzimmer im oberen Teil ab, was ermöglicht, dass das Licht das Schlafzimmer durchflutet, wenn der Vorhang zurückgezogen ist.

Une grande baie vitrée sépare la chambre située à l'étage, ce qui permet à la lumière de remplir la chambre lorsque le rideau est ouvert.

Un gran cristal separa el dormitorio ubicado en la parte superior, lo que permite que la luz llene el dormitorio cuando la cortina está recogida.

One of the loft's *leitmotivs* is the decorative wooden structure that separates the entryway from the living room; its design is replicated on the ceiling over the bed.

Eines der Leitmotive dieses Lofts ist die dekorative Holzstruktur, die den Eingang vom Wohnzimmer abtrennt und sich in der Decke über dem Bett wiederholt.

Un des leitmotive du loft est la structure en bois décorative qui sépare l'entrée du séjour et qui est copiée au plafond au-dessus du lit.

Uno de los leitmotiv del loft es la estructura de madera decorativa que separa la entrada de la sala de estar, y que es replicada en el techo de encima la cama.

RADIO LOFT

85 m² | 914.60 sq ft

~~~~~

INBLUM

~~~~~

VILNUS, LITHUANIA

~~~~~

© ANDREJS NIKIFOROVS

The result of experimentation with ideas, materials and solutions, this loft, located in a former radio manufacturing space, is one of the first open concept spaces designed as such in the city. Because of the clear unobstructed space the building had inherited from the building's industrial past, it was necessary to devise an open plan for all the functional zones. In addition, the industrial elements defining the space, such as the wooden roof beams, and the concrete beams that cross the space both horizontally and vertically, have been left exposed.

Als Ergebnis des Experimentierens mit Ideen, Materialien und Lösungen war dieser Loft, der in einer alten Fabrik zur Herstellung von Radios liegt, einer der ersten offenen Räume der Stadt, der als solcher konzipiert wurde. Der durchscheinende Bereich, der vom industriellen Ursprung des Gebäudes definiert wird, zwingt den Gestalter, die Funktionszonen komplett offen zu planen. Ebenso wird entschieden, alle industriellen Elemente, die den Raum definieren, sichtbar zu lassen, wie etwa die Deckenbalken und die Betonbalken, die den Raum horizontal und vertikal kreuzen.

Fruit de l'expérimentation des idées, matériaux et solutions, ce loft, situé dans un ancien atelier de fabrication de radios, est un des premiers espaces ouverts conçus comme tels dans la ville. L'espace ouvert défini par l'origine industrielle du bâtiment oblige à planifier les espaces fonctionnels de manière totalement ouverte. Il a également été décidé de laisser tous les éléments industriels qui définissent l'espace tels que les poutres du plafond et celles en béton qui croisent l'espace à l'horizontale et à la verticale.

Fruto de la experimentación de ideas, materiales y soluciones, este loft, ubicado en un antiguo taller de fabricación de radios, es uno de los primeros espacios abiertos concebidos como tal de la ciudad. El área diáfana definida por el origen industrial del edificio obliga a planificar las zonas funcionales de forma totalmente abierta. También se decide dejar expuestos todos los elementos industriales que definen el espacio, como son las vigas del techo y las de hormigón que cruzan el espacio en horizontal y vertical.

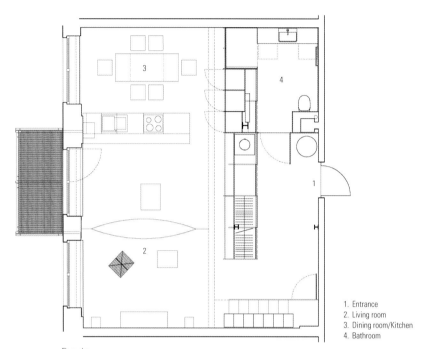

Floor plan

1. Entrance
2. Living room
3. Dining room/Kitchen
4. Bathroom

The ductwork is exposed, and the lighting fixtures that were selected increase the industrial atmosphere.

Die sichtbaren Rohrleitungen werden erhalten, und die Einrichtung, die für die Beleuchtung ausgewählt wird, trägt dazu bei, das Gefühl eines Fabrik-Looks noch zu steigern.

Les canalisations apparentes ont été conservées et la décoration choisie pour l'éclairage contribue à augmenter la sensation de cadre industriel.

Se conservan las cañerías al descubierto y la decoración escogida en iluminación contribuye a incrementar la sensación de ambiente industrial.

Taking advantage of the high industrial ceiling, the space is divided into two levels; the bedroom is upstairs, and the day zone and bathroom are below.

Der Raum wird in zwei Ebenen aufgeteilt, indem der Planer die in der Industrie übliche Deckenhöhe ausnutzt. In der oberen Etage befindet sich das Schlafzimmer, in der unteren Etage sind Aufenthaltsbereich und Bad untergebracht.

L'espace est réparti sur deux niveaux en profitant de la hauteur du plafond industriel : à l'étage supérieur se trouve la chambre tandis que l'espace de vie et la salle de bains sont à l'étage inférieur.

El espacio está dividido en dos niveles, aprovechando la altura del techo industrial, y en la parte superior encontramos el dormitorio mientras que en el primer nivel se ubica la zona de día y el baño.

WORKSHOP
TURNED INTO LOFT

90 m² | 968.75 sq ft

———

JOSEP CANO

———

BARCELONA, SPAIN

———

© NICOLÁS FOTOGRAFÍA

This project converts a hundred-year-old watchmaking shop into a welcoming loft. The choice was made to retain the dual function of the space, preserve the living and working environments, and hide the kitchen and bathroom; but always to maintain a clear and expansive open space. The structure, now that it is landscaped, presents spatial and visual continuity all the way from the terrace in the front to the sleeping space, which is separated from the rest by curtains.

Eine jahrhundertealte ehemalige Uhrmacherwerkstatt wird bei diesem Projekt in einen gemütlichen Loft umgewandelt. Der Architekt hat sich entschieden, die funktionale Dualität des Raumes aufrechtzuerhalten und den Wohn- und Arbeitsbereich zu bewahren, während Küche und Bad verborgen werden, wobei jedoch jederzeit ein durchscheinender und klarer Raum erhalten bleibt. Die Struktur in Querformat zeigt eine räumliche und visuelle Kontinuität von der Vorderseite, wo sich eine Terrasse befindet, bis hin zu dem Raum, der als Schlafzimmer dient und von der übrigen Wohnung durch Vorhänge abgetrennt wird.

Un ancien atelier d'horlogerie centenaire transforme ce projet en un loft accueillant. On a opté pour le maintien de la dualité fonctionnelle de l'espace et la conservation de l'espace de vie et de travail en dissimulant la cuisine et la salle de bains tout en conservant à tout moment un espace ouvert et clair. La structure apaisée présente une continuité spatiale et visuelle depuis la partie avant où se trouve une terrasse qui va jusqu'à la partie nuit, séparée du reste par des rideaux.

Un antiguo taller de relojería centenario se transforma en este proyecto en un acogedor loft. Se opta por mantener la dualidad funcional del espacio, y conservar el ambiente para vivir y para trabajar, escondiendo la cocina y el baño, pero manteniendo en todo momento un espacio diáfano y claro. La estructura apaisada presenta una continuidad espacial y visual desde la parte frontal, donde se encuentra una terraza, hasta el espacio destinado a habitación, separado del resto por unas cortinas.

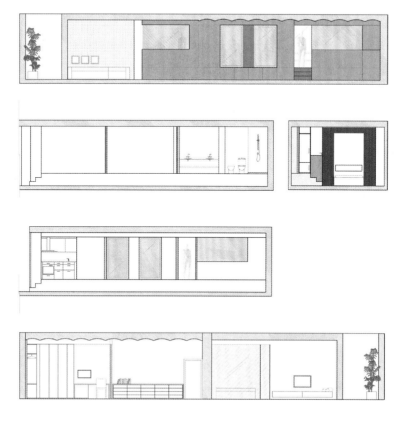

Sections

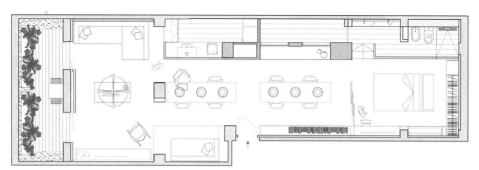

Floor plan

The structural elements are placed in such a way as to leave most of the space open and uncluttered; this allows the loft to be used most appropriately for each occasion.

Die Anordnung der strukturellen Elemente lässt den größten Teil des Raumes durchscheinend und frei, wirken um dem Loft je nach Augenblick die am besten passende Nutzung zu geben.

La disposition des éléments structurels laisse une grande partie de l'espace ouvert et libre pour conférer au loft l'usage le plus approprié selon le moment.

La disposición de los elementos estructurales dejan la mayor parte del espacio diáfano y libre, para darle al loft el uso más adecuado dependiendo del momento.

The decision was made to increase the loft's versatility by raising the bathroom and kitchen to a higher level, starting at the height of the interior courtyard, and placing one on either side.

Hier beschloss der Planer, Bad und Küche auf eine höhere Ebene anzuheben, ausgehend von der Höhe des Innenhofes, und an jeweils einer Seite zu platzieren, um die vielseitige Verwendbarkeit des Lofts zu verstärken.

Il a été décidé de surélever la salle de bains et la cuisine à un niveau supérieur en partant de la hauteur de la cour intérieure en les plaçant de chaque côté afin de renforcer la versatilité du loft.

Se decide elevar el baño y la cocina a un nivel superior partiendo de la altura del patio interior, situándolos uno a cada lado, para reforzar la versatilidad del loft.

SP
LOFT

91 m² | 979.52 sq ft

—

SADAR+VUGA

—

LJUBLJANA, SLOVENIA

—

© MIRAN KAMBIČ

Remodeled loft in a nineteenth century house in the city center. The goal of the architects is to seek contrasting effects and sensations. The result is a house that comingles historic and current styles, and is simultaneously warm and cool, open and closed. The threads that tie it all together are the aluminum rails that span the ceilings. They suspend sliding doors that can isolate the kitchen, bedroom, bathroom, or dressing room. When these doors are open, the living environment extends from the living/dining room to the bedroom and bath.

Renovierter Loft in einem Haus aus dem 19. Jahrhundert im Stadtzentrum. Das Architekturbüro beabsichtigt, Effekte und Empfindungen einander gegenüberzustellen, so dass eine gleichzeitig warme und kalte Wohnstätte entsteht, die zugleich offen und geschlossen ist und in der sich die Stile aus Vergangenheit und Gegenwart mischen. Wie ein roter Faden ziehen sich die Deckenbalken aus Aluminium durch die gesamte Wohnstätte. Küche, Schlafzimmer, Bad und Ankleidezimmer werden von Schiebetüren abgegrenzt, die an den Balken hängen. Werden sie geöffnet, dehnt sich der Wohnraum von Wohn-Esszimmer auf Schlafzimmer und Bad aus.

Loft rénové dans un bâtiment du XIXᵉ s. du centre-ville. Le cabinet cherche à opposer des effets et sensations en offrant comme résultat un logement à la fois chaleureux et froid, ouvert et fermé, où se mélangent des styles d'hier et d'aujourd'hui. Les poteaux en aluminium du plafond sont le fil conducteur de toute l'habitation. La cuisine, la chambre, la salle de bains et le dressing sont délimités par des portes coulissantes qui sont suspendues. En les ouvrant, l'espace de vie s'étend du salon-salle à manger à la chambre et salle de bains.

Loft reformado en una casa del siglo XIX del centro de la ciudad. El estudio busca contraponer efectos y sensaciones, dando como resultado una vivienda cálida a la par que fría, abierta y cerrada, donde se mezclan estilos del pasado y actuales. Las vigas de aluminio del techo son el hilo conductor de toda la vivienda. La cocina, la habitación, baño y vestidor están delimitados por puertas correderas que cuelgan de ellas. Abriéndolas, se extiende el espacio vital desde el salón comedor a la habitación y el baño.

The living room is a reinterpretation of an Art Nouveau sitting room, dominated by a ceiling mirror that resembles a fresco reflecting the components of the room.

Dieses Wohnzimmer ist die Neuinterpretation eines Wohnzimmers im Art Nouveau-Stil, dominiert von einem Spiegel an der Decke, in dem sich alle darin befindlichen Elemente spiegeln, als handele es sich um eine Freske.

Le séjour est une réinterprétation d'un salon Art Nouveau présidé par un miroir au plafond dans lequel se reflètent tous les éléments qui le composent comme s'il s'agissait d'une fresque.

La sala de estar es una reinterpretación de un salón Art Noveau presidido por un espejo en el techo en el que se reflejan todos los elementos que lo componen como si de un fresco se tratara.

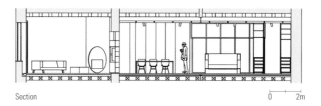

Section

0   2m

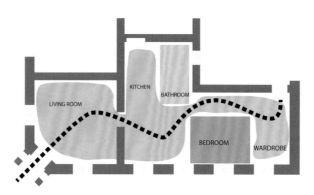

Functional diagram

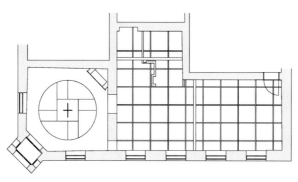

Reflected ceiling plan

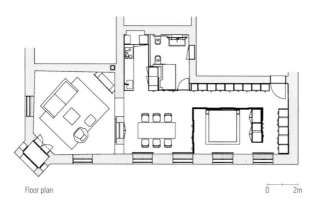

Floor plan

0   2m

When they sliding doors are shut orderly, functional spaces are created. When they are opened, one encounters very distinct visual experiences: from industrial to vintage, and from grounded to ethereal.

Durch Schließen der Schiebetüren werden geordnete und funktionale Wohnräume geschaffen. Werden sie geöffnet, macht der Betrachter äußerst unterschiedliche visuelle Erfahrungen: vom Industriellen zu Vintage, vom Himmlischen zum Irdischen.

En fermant les portes coulissantes, on a créé des espaces ordonnés et fonctionnels. Si on les ouvre, cela créé des expériences visuelles très différentes : de l'industriel au vintage, de l'éthéré au terrestre.

Cerrando las puertas correderas se crean espacios ordenados y funcionales. Si se abren, encontramos experiencias visuales muy distintas: de lo industrial a lo *vintage*, de lo etéreo a lo terrenal.

In the floor plan, the apartment has added breadth in its central zone; this provides enough space to locate the kitchen and bathroom opposite the living/dining room. The siding doors allow these rooms to be revealed or concealed as desired.

Man nutzt die Geräumigkeit, welche der Grundriss der Wohnung in der Mitte gewinnt, um Küche und Bad gegenüber dem Esszimmer zu platzieren. Dank der Schiebetüren lassen sich die Räume nach Belieben verbergen oder zeigen.

On profite de l'espace conféré à l'étage de l'appartement au niveau de sa partie centrale afin de situer la cuisine et la salle de bains en face de la salle à manger. Les portes coulissantes permettent de dissimuler ou de montrer ces pièces à volonté.

Se aprovecha la amplitud que adquiere la planta del apartamento en su parte central, para situar la cocina y el baño frente a la sala comedor. Las puertas correderas contribuyen a ocultar o a mostrar estas estancias a voluntad.

BACHELOR
PAD

93 m² | 1,000 sq ft

—

FALKEN REYNOLDS

—

VANCOUVER, BRITISH COLUMBIA, CANADA

—

© MARTIN TESSLER & LUCAS FINLAY

This loft is located in a hundred-year-old former warehouse. This makeover juxtaposes industrial and sophisticated elements; cement flooring meets brick walls; raw concrete stands out against walnut timbers and stainless steel appliances. The house is soundproofed against the noises of the city, and it is completely automated. Since there are windows on only one side of the apartment, a complex LED lighting system helps created the required atmosphere.

Dieser Loft befindet sich in einem hundertjährigen Gebäude, das einst ein Lager beherbergte. In einem Nebeneinander von Industriellem und Raffinesse vermischen sich Zementböden mit Backsteinwänden, grober Beton und Material wie Walnussholz oder das Edelstahl der elektrischen Haushaltsgeräte. Das Haus ist schalldicht, von der Hektik der Stadt abgeschirmt und komplett mit Haustechnik ausgestattet. Da die Wohnung nur nach einer Seite Fenster hat, trägt ein ausgefeiltes LED-Beleuchtungssystem dazu bei, das passende Ambiente zu schaffen.

Ce loft se trouve dans un bâtiment centenaire qui abritait autrefois un entrepôt. Dans une juxtaposition entre l'industriel et la sophistication, se mélangent les sols en ciment et les murs de brique, le béton brut et les matériaux tels que le noyer ou l'acier inoxydable des appareils domestiques. Le loft est insonorisé et isolé de l'agitation de la ville et entièrement domotique. Comme l'appartement a des fenêtres d'un seul côté, un système sophistiqué d'éclairage LED contribue à créer l'ambiance adéquate.

Este loft se ubica en un edificio centenario que albergaba un almacén. En una yuxtaposición entre lo industrial y la sofisticación, se mezclan suelos de cemento con paredes de ladrillo, hormigón en bruto y materiales como el nogal o el acero inoxidable de los electrodomésticos. La casa está insonorizada y aislada del bullicio de la ciudad, y es totalmente domótica. Debido a que el apartamento tiene ventanas a un solo lado, un sofisticado sistema de iluminación LED contribuye a crear el ambiente adecuado.

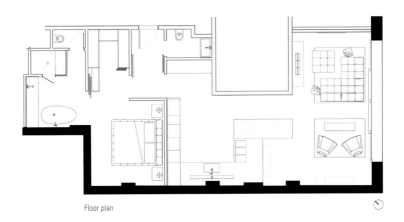

Floor plan

The space has been designed to reflect
the owner's qualities; he is a unique,
unconventional person, and so the spaces
and materials reflect his personality.

Entsprechend dem Charakter des Eigentümers,
einer besonderen und wenig herkömmlichen
Person, wurde der Raum so konzipiert, dass sich
Räume und Materialien in seine Persönlichkeit
hineinversetzen.

L'espace a été conçu selon le caractère du
propriétaire, une personne spéciale et peu
conventionnelle, de sorte que les espaces et
matériaux s'identifient à sa personnalité.

El espacio ha sido concebido de acuerdo al
carácter del propietario, alguien especial
y poco convencional, de forma que los espacios
y materiales se identifican con su personalidad.

VILA
MATILDE

95 m² | 1,022.57 sq ft

—

TERRA E TUMA

—

VILA MATILDE SÃO PAULO, BRAZIL

—

© PEDRO KOK

Before it was remodeled, this house on the outskirts of the city had serious structural and sanitation problems. Because it was in an advanced stage of deterioration, it had to be rebuilt in the shortest time possible. The architects' studio took advantage of its experience with block structure to save time and money. The greatest challenge was to grapple with the structural problems in the neighboring buildings. This project was selected to represent Brazil in the 2016 International Architectural Exposition in Venice.

Vor der Umgestaltung hatte dieses Haus, das im Randbezirk der Hauptstadt steht, ernste bauliche und sanitärtechnische Probleme und zeigte einen Verfall im fortge-schrittenen Zustand, weshalb es notwendig war, es in der geringstmöglichen Zeit zu renovieren. Das Architektenbüro nutzt seine Erfahrung im Einsatz von Mauern aus Ze-mentsteinen, um Zeit und Kosten zu optimieren. Die größte Herausforderung besteht darin, mit den baulichen Problemen der benachbarten Bauten zu kämpfen. Dieses Projekt wurde ausgewählt, Brasilien bei der Biennale von Venedig 2016 zu vertreten.

Avant les travaux, ce loft situé dans un quartier périphérique de la ville, avait de sé-rieux problèmes structurels et sanitaires, avec un état de détérioration avancé, ce qui a nécessité de le rénover au plus vite. Le cabinet profite de son expérience dans l'utilisation de la structure des blocs afin d'optimiser le temps et réduire les coûts. Le plus grand défi a été de surmonter les problèmes structurels des constructions avoisinantes. Ce projet a été choisi pour représenter le Brésil lors de la Biennale de Venise en 2016.

Antes de su reforma, esta vivienda situada en un barrio periférico de la metrópolis, tenía serios problemas estructurales y sanitarios y mostraba un avanzado estado de deterioro, por lo que había que reformarla en el menor tiempo posible. El estudio apro-vecha su experiencia en el uso de la estructura de bloques para optimizar tiempo y costes. El mayor reto es lidiar con los problemas estructurales de las construcciones vecinas. Este proyecto ha sido seleccionado para representar a Brasil en la Bienal de Venecia del 2016.

The lower floor holds the living room, bathroom, kitchen, laundry, and a suite. An inner courtyard that provides light and ventilation links the front and back sections of the home.

Im Erdgeschoss befinden sich Wohnzimmer, Bad, Küche, Hauswirtschaftsraum und ein Schlafzimmer mit Bad. Ein Innenhof, der für Licht und Belüftung sorgt, verbindet den vorderen Teil mit dem hinteren Teil der Wohnstätte.

Au rez-de-chaussée se trouvent le séjour, la salle de bains, la cuisine, la buanderie et une suite parentale. Une cour intérieure qui offre de la lumière et de l'air, relie les parties avant et arrière du loft.

En la planta inferior encontramos la sala de estar, el baño, cocina, lavandería y una suite. Un patio interior que proporciona luz y ventilación, articula la parte delantera con la parte trasera de la vivienda.

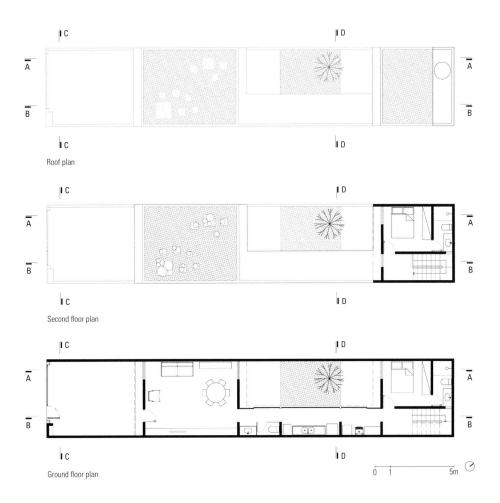

C

D

A

B

A

B

C

D

Roof plan

C

D

A

B

A

B

C

D

Second floor plan

C

D

A

B

A

B

C

D

Ground floor plan

0 1   5m

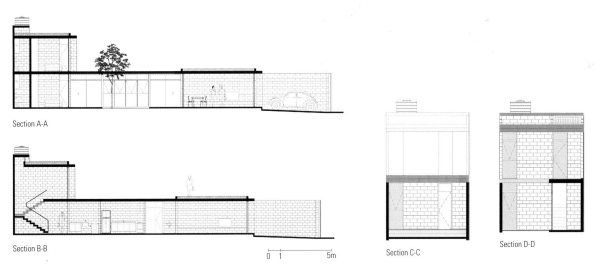

Section A-A

Section B-B

0 1   5m

Section C-C

Section D-D

The second floor has a guest room, and, right above the living room, there is a garden, which may be roofed over in the future if the family so desires.

Auf der zweiten Etage befindet sich ein Gästezimmer, und knapp über dem Wohnzimmer liegt ein Garten, der künftig überdacht werden kann, falls die Familie diesen Bereich benötigt.

Le premier étage comprend une chambre d'amis et juste au-dessus du séjour, se trouve un jardin qui pourra être couvert à l'avenir si la famille le souhaite.

La segunda planta incluye una habitación de invitados y justo encima de la sala de estar, encontramos un jardín, que podrá ser cubierto en un futuro si la familia lo necesita.

LOFT WITH
BRICKS AND WOOD

99 m² | 1,065.63 sq ft

—

MIKOŁAJSKASTUDIO COOPERATION WITH ARCHITECT GABRIELA OBŁOŃSKA

—

KATOWICE, POLAND

—

© MEBEL & STYL

This loft in the heart of the city is the result of the synergy between simplicity and industrial elements. The roughness of the precious and natural materials, such as wood and steel, mingle with the warmth and softness of the weavings, carpets, and upholstery. The smooth gray of the surfaces is broken by occasional details of solid black. Likewise, the textures of brick and unfinished plaster are juxtaposed with the smoothness of ceramics, glass, and varnished surfaces.

Dieser Loft im Herzen der Stadt ist eine Synergie zwischen Einfachheit und industriellen Elementen. Hier vermischt sich die Rauheit von natürlichen und edlen Materialien, wie Holz und Stahl, mit der Wärme der weichen Gewebe von Teppichen und Polsterung. Das Grau der glatten Oberflächen wird von Details in Schwarz unterbrochen. Auf gleiche Weise werden der Backstein und die Texturen von unbearbeitetem Gips neben glatter Keramik, Glas und lackierten Oberflächen angeordnet.

Ce loft au cœur de la ville est une synergie entre la simplicité et les éléments industriels. La rugosité des matériaux naturels et nobles tels que le bois et l'acier se mélange à la chaleur des tissus tendres des tapis et de la tapisserie. Le gris des surfaces lisses rompt avec les détails en noir. De la même manière, ont été juxtaposées la brique et les textures en plâtre sans terminer avec de la céramique lisse, du verre et des surfaces vernies.

Este loft en el corazón de la ciudad es una sinergia entre simplicidad y elementos industriales. Encontramos mezclados la rugosidad de los materiales naturales y nobles, como la madera y el acero, con la calidez de los tejidos blandos de alfombras y tapicería. El gris de las superficies lisas se rompe con detalles en color negro. De la misma forma, se yuxtaponen el ladrillo y texturas de yeso sin terminar con cerámica lisa, vidrio y superficies barnizadas.

The living room, with its imposing exposed structural wall, faces a private garden that provides a peaceful enclave in the heart of the bustling capital.

Das Wohnzimmer, in dem sich eine unverputzte Backsteinwand besonders hervorhebt, führt in einen Garten, der eine ruhige und friedliche Enklave inmitten der Hektik der Hauptstadt ist.

Le séjour dans lequel on distingue un mur de pierre apparente, donne sur un jardin privatif qui est une enclave tranquille et pacifique au milieu de l'agitation de la capitale.

La sala de estar, en la que destaca una pared de obra vista, da a un jardín privado que es un tranquilo y pacífico enclave en medio del bullicio de la capital.

The combination bedroom and bathroom is planned as a private area where the owners can relax. The bathroom mirrors reflect the exposed wall of the bedroom, accentuating the mix of contrast and continuity that relates the rooms and materials to each other.

Die Kombination von Schlafzimmer und Badezimmer ist als privater Bereich gedacht, in dem sich die Eigentümer entspannen können. Die Spiegel im Bad reflektieren die unverputzte Mauer im Schlafzimmer und betonen den Kontrast sowie die Kontinuität zwischen Räumen und Materialien.

La combinaison de la chambre avec la salle de bains a été conçue pour être l'espace privatif où les propriétaires peuvent se reposer. Les miroirs de la salle de bains reflètent le mur de pierre de la chambre accentuant ainsi le contraste et la continuité entre les cadres et les matériaux.

La combinación de la habitación con el cuarto de baño está pensada para ser el área privada donde los propietarios puedan relajarse. Los espejos del baño reflejan la pared de obra de la habitación, acentuando el contraste y la continuidad entre ambientes y materiales.

GO & JO
LOFTS

100 m² | 1,076.4 sq ft

FEDERICO DELROSSO

MILAN, ITALY

© MATEO PIAZZA

An old industrial building is used to create a pair of near-identical lofts for two brothers. For optimum use of the space, each dwelling has two levels. The second floor is a raised platform that is independent of the perimeter walls; it is supported on metal structures so as to have no impact on the overall four-story building. The railings separating the upper and lower floors are a continuation of the roof beams.

In einem ehemaligen Gewerbegebäude wurden zwei praktisch identische Lofts für zwei Brüder geschaffen. In beiden Fällen wurden zwei Ebenen eingerichtet, um den Bereich maximal auszunutzen. Die zweite Ebene ist eine unabhängig erhöhte Plattform, abgetrennt von den perimetralen Wänden, die so auf dem Metalltragewerk aufliegt, dass es die Gesamtheit des vierstöckigen Gebäudes nicht beeinflusst. Die Geländer, die den oberen Teil vom unteren trennen, sind letztendlich eine Fortsetzung der Dachsparren.

Dans un ancien bâtiment industriel, deux lofts ont été créés pratiquement à l'identique pour deux frères. Chaque espace est composé de deux niveaux afin de profiter au maximum de la surface. Le deuxième niveau est une plateforme surélevée de manière indépendante et séparée des murs périphériques qui repose sur des structures métalliques de sorte à ne pas affecter l'ensemble du bâtiment sur quatre étages. Les barrières qui séparent la partie supérieure de l'inférieure sont la continuité des poutres du plafond.

En un antiguo edificio de uso industrial se crean dos lofts prácticamente idénticos para dos hermanos. En cada espacio se establecen dos niveles de altura para aprovechar al máximo el área. La segunda planta es una plataforma alzada de forma independiente y separada de las paredes perimetrales que se apoya en unas estructuras de metal de manera que no afecta al conjunto del edificio de cuatro plantas. Las barandillas que separan la parte superior de la inferior vienen a ser una continuación de las vigas del techo.

The optical illusion created by the railings mimicking the beam becomes the apartment's key characteristic, because it ends up being a sort of spine that supports the different spaces and functions.

Das trügerische Spiel, das die Geländer hier spielen, indem sie den Balken nacheifern, wird zum grundlegenden Merkmal dieser Wohnstätte, denn letztendlich ist es eine Art Rückgrat, das Räume und Funktionen verwaltet.

Le jeu d'illusion que créent les barrières en simulant les poutres devient la principale caractéristique de l'habitation et finit par être une sorte de colonne vertébrale qui gère les espaces et fonctions.

El juego ilusorio que crean las barandillas emulando las vigas se convierte en la característica principal de la vivienda, pues acaba siendo una especie de columna vertebral que gestiona espacios y funciones.

Another feature is the manner in which the exposed brick walls, which hearken back to the original design, contrast with the other walls, which are plastered and painted.

Ein weiteres charakteristisches Merkmal der Wohnstätte ist der Kontrast zwischen den unverputzten Backsteinwänden, die das ursprüngliche Industriedesign würdigen, und den angestrichenen und durchwirkten Wänden.

Un autre élément caractéristique de l'habitation est le contraste entre les murs de brique apparente respectant la conception industrielle d'origine avec les murs peints et gâchés.

Otro de los elementos característicos de la vivienda es el contraste entre las paredes de ladrillo visto, respetando el diseño industrial original, con las paredes pintadas y amasadas.

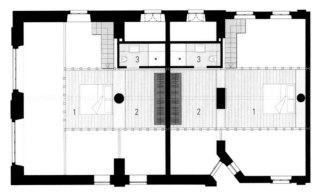

1. Bed
2. Wardrobe
3. Bathroom

Second floor plan. Left, Jo Loft . Right, Go Loft

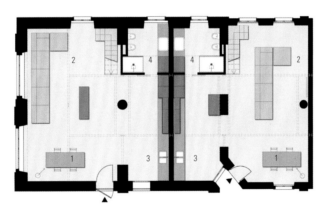

1. Dining room
2. Living room
3. Kitchen
4. Bathroom

Ground floor plan. Left, Jo Loft. Right, Go Loft

The two lofts are designed to be almost identical, except that the upper floor in the right loft is larger, for structural reasons.

Die Gestaltung beider Lofts wurde praktisch gleichmäßig konzipiert, mit Ausnahme der oberen Etage, die bei dem Loft rechts aufgrund baulicher Elemente etwas mehr Oberfläche hat.

Le design des deux lofts est conçu pratiquement de manière équivalente, à l'exception de l'étage supérieur qui, dans celui de droite, dispose d'un peu plus de surface en raison des éléments structurels.

El diseño de los dos lofts es concebido prácticamente de forma equitativa, a excepción de la planta superior, que en el de la derecha tiene un poco más de superficie debido a elementos estructurales.

The location of the structural spine is another element that differs between the two homes. In the Jo loft it is almost in the center of the space, and in the Go loft it is practically attached to the wall.

Der Standort der tragenden Säule ist ein weiteres Element, das die beiden Wohnungen voneinander unterscheidet. Während sie sich im Loft Jo fast in der Mitte des Raumes befindet, steht sie im LoftGo praktisch direkt an der Wand.

L'emplacement de la colonne structurelle est un autre des éléments distincts entre les deux lofts. Tandis que le loft de Jo se trouve pratiquement au centre de l'espace, celui de Go reste pratiquement collé au mur.

La ubicación de la columna estructural es otro de los elementos distintivos entre las dos viviendas. Mientras que en el Loft Jo se encuentra casi en el centro del espacio, en el Loft Go queda prácticamente pegada a la pared.

The project seeks to emphasize the cohesion between the two spaces, as well as their unique architectural mix of conservatism and modernity.

Das Projekt möchte gleichzeitig den Zusammenhang zwischen den beiden Räumen und deren Melange aus konservativ und modern betonen.

Le projet souhaite souligner la cohésion entre les deux espaces et leur mélange à la fois conservateur et contemporain.

El proyecto quiere resaltar la cohesión entre los dos espacios, y su mezcla conservadora y contemporánea a la vez.

Height is added to the upper floor walls, which measure only 2.1 meters, by placing cut glass beside the stone walls and structural columns.

Neben Steinwänden und Tragsäulen wird geschliffenes Glas platziert, um der unteren Ebene mit nur 2,10 m Höhe Vertikalität zu verleihen.

À proximité des murs de pierre et des colonnes structurelles se trouve du verre coupé pour donner de la verticalité au niveau supérieur à seulement 2,10 mètres de hauteur.

Al lado de las paredes de piedra y las columnas estructurales se coloca vidrio cortado para dar verticalidad a la planta superior, de solo 2,10 metros de altura.

INDUSTRIAL LOFT

100 m² | 1,076.39 sq ft

———

DIEGO REVOLLO

———

SÃO PAULO, BRAZIL

———

© ALAIN BRUGIER

This loft blends its industrial quality with contemporary comfort and design. The combination of grey and black tones emphasizes the masculinity of the space, and reflects the personality of the owner. The idea was to integrate the two separate spaces into just one two-tiered space. On the lower floor, the kitchen, living room, and dining room fit together perfectly: the wooden table is built into the kitchen cabinet, and nudges us on into the living room. Above are the open bedroom and bath.

Dieser Loft kombiniert seinen Industriecharakter mit modernem Komfort und Design. Die Kombination von Grau- und Schwarztönen beabsichtigt, die den maskulinen Charakter des Raumes als Reflexion der Persönlichkeit des Eigentümers zu betonen. Die verschiedenen Räume sollen zu einem einzigen Raum auf zwei Ebenen integriert werden. Auf der unteren Etage sind Küche, Wohnzimmer und Esszimmer perfekt integriert: Der Holztisch ist in das Küchenmobiliar eingebunden und weist uns Richtung Wohnzimmer. In einem offenen Bereich auf der oberen Etage befinden sich Schlafzimmer und Bad.

Ce loft combine le caractère industriel avec le confort et le design contemporains. La combinaison des tons gris et noirs prétend accentuer la masculinité de l'espace comme un reflet de la personnalité du propriétaire. On a recherché à intégrer divers espaces dans un seul espace à deux niveaux. Au rez-de-chaussée, la cuisine, le séjour et la salle à manger sont parfaitement intégrés : la table en bois est intégrée au meuble de cuisine et nous transfère dans le séjour. À l'étage supérieur se trouvent la chambre et la salle de bains, toutes deux ouvertes.

Este loft combina el carácter industrial con el confort y el diseño contemporáneos. La combinación de tonos grises y negros pretenden emfatizar la masculinidad del espacio, como un reflejo de la personalidad del propietario. Se ha buscado la intregración de los distintos espacios en una única en dos niveles. En el piso inferior, la cocina, la sala y el comedor estén perfectamente integrados: la mesa de madera está integrada en el mueble de cocina, y nos lanza hacia la sala de estar. En el piso superior, abiertos, se hallan el dormitorio y el baño.

Beyond the matter of its structure, the contemporary element is present in the furniture and all the decorative details. The goal here is to achieve a typically "New York" look.

Über seine Struktur hinaus ist das zeitgenössische Element in allen dekorativen Details anwesend. Das Zeitgenössische findet sich sowohl im Mobiliar als in den übrigen Dekoelementen wieder, wodurch der typisch New Yorker Look erzielt wird.

Au-delà de sa structure, l'élément contemporain est présent dans toute la décoration, la modernité est présente aussi bien dans le mobilier que dans le reste des éléments de décoration afin d'obtenir un air typiquement new-yorkais.

Más allá de su estructura, el elemento contemporáneo está presente en todos los detalles ornamentales, la contemporaneidad está presente tanto en el mobiliario, como el resto de elementos ornamentales, con el fin de lograr el aire típicamente neoyorkino.

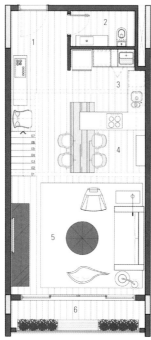

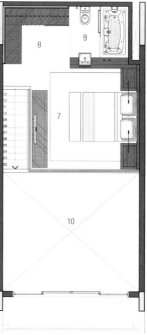

Lower floor plan

Upper floor plan

1. Entry hall
2. Powder room
3. Kitchen
4. Dining area
5. Living area
6. Terrace
7. Bedroom
8. Bathroom
9. Dressing area
10. Open to below

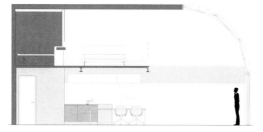

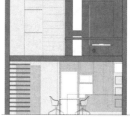

Cross section

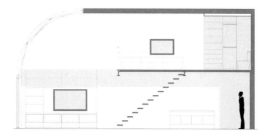

Longitudinal sections

The pine wood dining room table is anchored into the kitchen cabinet; it works both to unite the two spaces, and to create a strongly modern effect.

Der Esszimmertisch aus Kiefernholz ist am Küchenschrank verankert, gleichzeitig soll er die beiden Räume verbinden, wodurch eine starke Modernität erzielt wird.

La table de salle à manger en pin est ancrée dans le meuble de la cuisine qui sert aussi de lien entre les deux espaces, conférant ainsi un effet de forte modernité.

La mesa del comedor, de madera de pino, está anclada en el mueble de cocina; a la vez que sirve para unificar los dos espacios, se consigue un un efecto de fuerte modernidad.

On the upper level, the divisions between bedroom and bathroom have been eliminated, leaving an ample and completely open space.

Auf der oberen Etage wurden die Abtrennungen zwischen Schlafzimmer und Bad beseitigt, dieser Bereich ist nun komplett offen, was dem Raum eine enorme Geräumigkeit verleiht.

À l'étage, les cloisons ont été retirées entre la chambre et la salle de bains, entièrement ouvertes, ce qui confère un espace plus grand.

En el nivel superior se han eliminado las separaciones entre el dormitorio y el baño, completamente abierto, lo que dota el espacio de gran amplitud.

BOX
117

103 m² | 1,108.68 sq ft

———

TIM DIEKHANS ARCHITEKTUR

———

BERLIN, GERMANY

———

© CHRISTIAN REISTER

This loft was built in a five-story Wilhelminian building from the early twentieth centu-ry; it is part of the rear courtyard of a factory. The kitchen, living room, and dining room share one space, which has access to an exterior balcony. The bedroom, bathroom, and toilet are essentially open to the air, separated as they are only by glass dividers. This grouping creates a space that is open, airy, and luminous.

Dieser Loft entstand in einem fünfstöckigen Gebäude im wilhelminischen Stil aus dem frühen 20. Jahrhundert und gehört zum Hinterhof einer Fabrik. Küche, Wohnzimmer und Esszimmer teilen sich den gleichen Raum mit Zugang zu einem Balkon nach au-ßen. Im gleichen Bereich sind Schlafzimmer, Bad und Toilette platziert, die praktisch in der Luft hängen und nur durch Glaswände abgetrennt sind. Das Ensemble bildet einen offenen, durchscheinenden und sehr hellen Raum.

Ce loft se trouve dans un bâtiment de cinq étages de style Wilhelminian du début du XXᵉ s. et appartient à la cour arrière d'une usine. La cuisine, le séjour et la salle à manger partagent un même espace, avec un accès à un balcon extérieur. Dans un même espace, la chambre, la salle de bains et les toilettes se trouvent pratiquement à l'air, uniquement séparés par des paravents en verre. L'ensemble forme un espace ouvert et très lumineux.

Este loft está construido en un edificio de cinco niveles de estilo Wilhelminian de prin-cipios del siglo XX y pertenece al patio trasero de una fábrica. Cocina, sala de estar y comedor comparten un mismo espacio, con acceso a un balcón exterior. En una misma zona se ubican dormitorio, baño y aseo que se encuentran prácticamente al aire, únicamente separados por mamparas de cristal. El conjunto forma un espacio abierto, diáfano y muy luminoso.

The kitchen cabinetry is hand crafted of antique wood, as is the hardware on the doors. Most of the decorative items were found in Berlin markets, and they provide the space with a homey feel.

Küchenmöbel und Türschließen sind aus altem Holz von Hand gefertigt. Die meisten dekorativen Elemente stammen von den Märkten Berlins und geben der Wohnung ein wohnliches Aussehen.

Les meubles de la cuisine sont fabriqués à la main avec du bois ancien tout comme les poignées de porte. La plupart des éléments de décoration proviennent des marchés de Berlin et confèrent un côté familial au bien.

Los muebles de la cocina están hechos a mano con madera antigua, al igual que los cierres de las puertas. La mayoría de elementos decorativos provienen de los mercados de Berlín, y confieren un aspecto hogareño a la vivienda.

The floor is made of cement that is clearly oily; this makes for a very clear contrast against the white surfaces of the walls, ceiling, and glazed ceramic tiles, thus maximizing the feeling of spaciousness.

Neben den weißen Oberflächen an Wänden, Decke und Glaskeramikfliesen erzielt der Boden aus mit Öllack versiegeltem Zement einen äußerst sauberen Gegensatz und maximiert das Gefühl von Geräumigkeit.

Le sol est en ciment clairement huileux avec les surfaces blanches des murs, le plafond et les carreaux en céramique vitrée, offre un contraste très clair et maximise la sensation d'espace.

El suelo es de cimiento claramente aceitoso junto a las superficies blancas de las paredes, el techo y las baldosas de cerámica vidriada, consigue un contraste muy limpio y maximiza la sensación de amplitud.

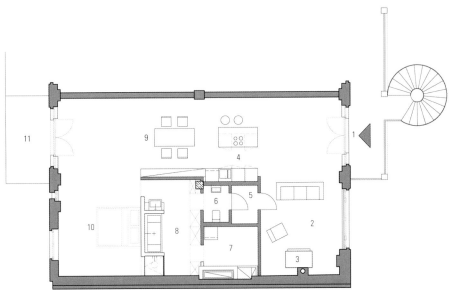

Floor plan

1. Entrance
2. Living area
3. Fireplace
4. Cooking area
5. Cloakroom
6. Toilet
7. Storeroom
8. Open Bathroom
9. Dining area
10. Sleeping area
11. Balcony

LOFT IN BRATISLAVA'S OLD TOWN

105 m² | 1,130.21 sq ft

—

LUKÁŠ KORDÍK, ŠTEFAN POLAKOVIČ,
SAMUEL ZEMAN, JANA BENKOVÁ / GUTGUT

—

BRATISLAVA, SLOVAKIA

—

© PETER ČINTALAN

This loft, in the city's historic district, is in a 1928 building designed by architect Clement Šilinger. The architects transform a four-room apartment into a multi-functional space for both living and working. The only divider in the dwelling is a functioning wall that works simultaneously as storage, a closet, laundry space, and a kitchen. The remodeled space retains the wooden doors and some of the flooring from the previous design.

Der Loft gehört zu einem Gebäude aus dem Jahr 1928 des Architekten Clement Šilinger, das im historischen Stadtzentrum liegt. Das Architektenbüro wandelt eine Wohnung mit vier Räumen in einen Multifunktionsraum um, in dem der Bewohner nicht nur lebt sondern auch arbeiten kann. Das einzige Trennelement der Wohnstätte ist eine Funktionswand, die gleichzeitig als Wandschrank, Waschraum, Stauraum und Küche fungiert. Beim Umbau blieben die Holztüren und Teile des Bodens des vorherigen Gestaltung erhalten.

Le loft se trouve dans un bâtiment de 1928 de l'architecte Clement Šilinger, situé dans le centre historique de la ville. Le cabinet transforme un appartement de quatre chambres en un espace multifonctionnel où il est possible d'y vivre et d'y travailler. Le seul élément de division de l'habitation est un mur fonctionnel qui sert à la fois d'armoire, de buanderie, de rangement et de cuisine. Les travaux ont prévu de conserver les portes en bois et certaines parties de l'ancien.

El loft pertenece a un edificio del año 1928 del arquitecto Clement Šilinger, situado en el centro histórico de la ciudad. El estudio transforma un apartamento de cuatro habitaciones en un espacio multifuncional donde vivir y también poder trabajar. El único elemento de división de la vivienda es un muro funcional que hace las veces de armario, espacio de lavandería, almacenaje y cocina al mismo tiempo. En la reforma, se mantienen las puertas de madera y partes del suelo del diseño anterior.

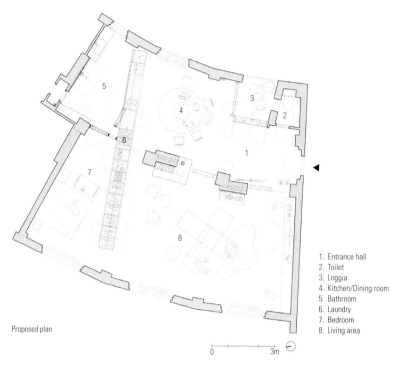

Proposed plan

1. Entrance hall
2. Toilet
3. Loggia
4. Kitchen/Dining room
5. Bathroom
6. Laundry
7. Bedroom
8. Living area

0   3m

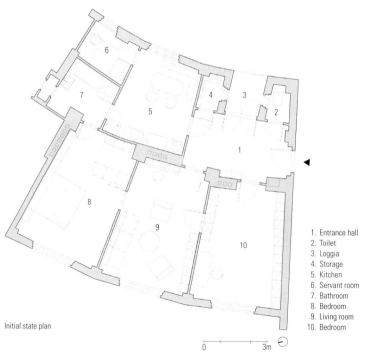

Initial state plan

1. Entrance hall
2. Toilet
3. Loggia
4. Storage
5. Kitchen
6. Servant room
7. Bathroom
8. Bedroom
9. Living room
10. Bedroom

0   3m

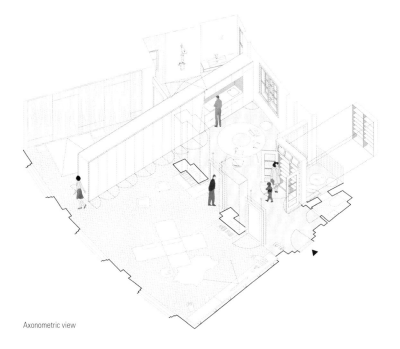

Axonometric view

Half of the flooring in the apartment is the
original oak parquet, and the other, from the
kitchen to the bathroom, is red vinyl.

Die Hälfte des Bodens der Wohnung ist altes
Eichenparkett und die andere Hälfte, von der
Küche bis zum Badezimmer, ist aus rotem
Gummi.

La moitié du sol de l'appartement est l'ancien
parquet en chêne et l'autre moitié, de la cuisine
à la salle de bains, est en gomme rouge.

La mitad del suelo del apartamento es el
antiguo parqué de roble y la otra mitad, desde
la cocina hasta el cuarto de baño, es de goma
roja.

The large mahogany kitchen table is a made of concentric circles glued together around a central opening, and resting on a metal base.

Der Küchentisch ist eine großes Gefüge aus Mahagoniholz, aus aneinander geklebten konzentrischen Kreisen mit einem Loch in der Mitte gefertigt, der auf einer Metallkonstruktion ruht.

La table de la cuisine est une grande structure en acajou en forme de cercles concentriques collés, avec un vide au milieu et qui repose sur une structure métallique.

La mesa de la cocina es una gran estructura de madera de caoba hecha de círculos concéntricos encolados, con un agujero en medio y que descansa sobre una construcción de metal.

On the dividing wall, the combination of white metal and wood creates a visual game in which materiality plays off against the penetration of light.

Die Kombination aus weißem Metall und Holz in der Trennwand schafft ein visuelles Spiel im Raum mit der Stofflichkeit und dem Einfall des Lichtes.

La combinaison du métal blanc et du bois sur le mur séparateur créé un jeu visuel dans l'espace avec la matérialité et la pénétration de la lumière.

La combinación de metal blanco y madera en la pared divisoria crea un juego visual en el espacio con la materialidad y la penetración de la luz.

GREY LOFT

110 m² | 1,183.60 sq ft

—

0000X ARCHITECTS

—

OSTROVSKÉHO, CZECH REPUBLIC

—

© MARTIN ZEMAN

In this two-story loft, materials for different surfaces are mixed, and run the gamut from white to pale gray. The size of the kitchen has been reduced to provide more room for moving around and for enlarging the access way through the French doors out to the terrace. For this same reason, a stainless steel island, which also functions as a dining table, has been added to the kitchen. On the other side is the bedroom, with a custom-made bed lit from below to create a floating effect.

Bei diesem Loft auf zwei Ebenen wurden die Materialien verschiedener Oberflächen vermischt, die in der Farbskala von Weiß bis zu einem warmen Grau reichen. Bei der Umgestaltung wurde die Küche verkürzt, wodurch Raum für mehr Bewegungsfreiheit gewonnen wurde und dem Zugang zur Terrasse durch Fenstertüren mehr Geräumigkeit verliehen. Mit dem gleichen Ziel wurde in der Küche eine Insel aus Edelstahl platziert, die auch als Esstisch fungiert. Auf der anderen Seite befindet sich das Schlafzimmer, das mit einem maßgefertigten Bett ausgestattet ist, das vom Boden aus beleuchtet wird, wodurch eine schwebende Wirkung erzielt wird.

Dans ce loft sur deux niveaux se mélangent les matériaux pour diverses surfaces qui vont d'un escalier blanc au gris chaud. Les travaux ont prévu de réduire la cuisine gagnant ainsi de l'espace pour se déplacer et donnant de l'espace pour accéder à la terrasse des portes de style français. À cette fin, un îlot en acier inoxydable a été ajouté dans la cuisine qui sert également de table à manger. De l'autre côté se trouve la chambre avec un lit sur mesure, éclairé depuis le sol créant ainsi un effet flottant.

En este loft de dos niveles se mezclan materiales para distintas superficies que van de una escalera de color del blanco al gris cálido. En la reforma se acorta la cocina, ganando espacio para moverse y dando amplitud al acceso a la terraza de puertas de estilo francés. Con este mismo fin se añade una isla de acero inoxidable a la cocina que hace las veces de mesa de comedor. Al otro lado encontramos la habitación, que dispone de una cama hecha a medida que se ilumina desde el suelo creando un efecto flotante.

Among the loft's key elements are the slanted roofs; also important are the creative uses made of the pre-existing structural components, such as the beams and exposed brick.

Zu den Hauptelementen des Lofts zählen die Dachschrägen und das Spiel mit den strukturellen Elementen, die bereits vorhanden waren, wie etwa Balken oder unverputzte Backsteinmauern.

Un des éléments principaux du loft est les plafonds inclinés et le jeu d'éléments structurels déjà existants tels que les poutres ou les murs de brique apparente.

Uno de los elementos principales del loft son los techos inclinados y cómo se juega con los elementos estructurales que ya existían, como las vigas o paredes de ladrillo visto.

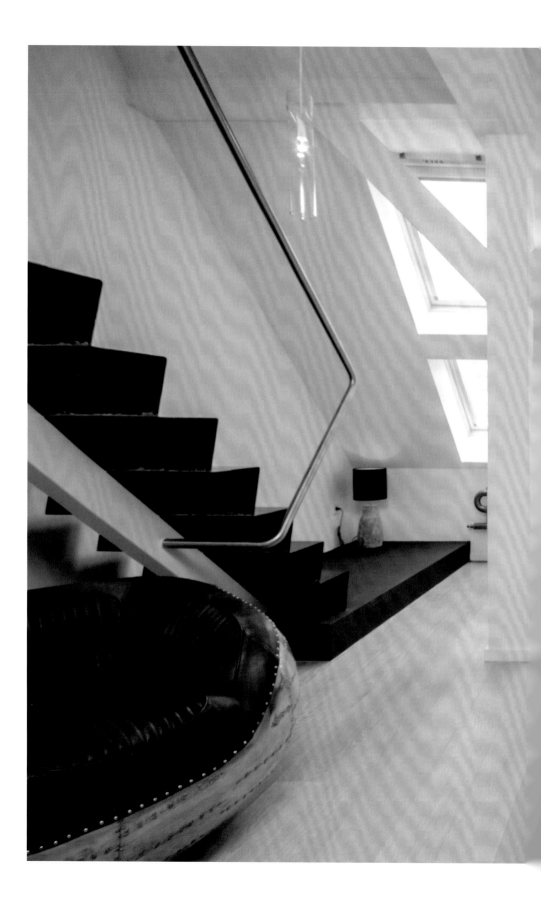

The upper level holds a study, or guest room, that overlooks the main space through a large glass divider; however, it has a curtain for privacy.

Im oberen Teil sehen wir ein Arbeitszimmer oder Gästezimmer, das durch eine große Glastür zum Hauptraum hin offen ist und einen Vorhang hat, um Privatsphäre zu gewinnen.

Au premier étage se trouve un bureau ou une chambre d'amis qui donne sur la chambre parentale grâce à une grande baie vitrée avec un rideau pour plus d'intimité.

En la parte superior encontramos un estudio o habitación para invitados, que está abierta a la habitación principal a través de una gran cristalera y dispone de una cortina para ganar privacidad.

The new stainless steel stairway is less steep than the previous one, and also serves as a bookshelf.

Die Treppe wird durch eine aus Edelstahl gefertigte Treppe mit einer geeigneteren und bequemeren Neigung ersetzt, die auch als Bücherregal dient.

L'ancien escalier a été remplacé par un autre avec une inclinaison plus appropriée et confortable, en acier inoxydable. Il sert également d'étagères pour livres.

Se reforma la escalera, reemplazando la anterior por otra con una inclinación más adecuada y confortable, hecha de acero inoxidable y que sirve también como estantería de libros.

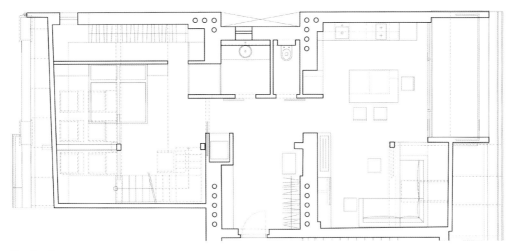

Upper floor plan

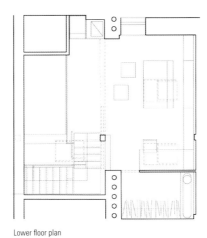

Lower floor plan

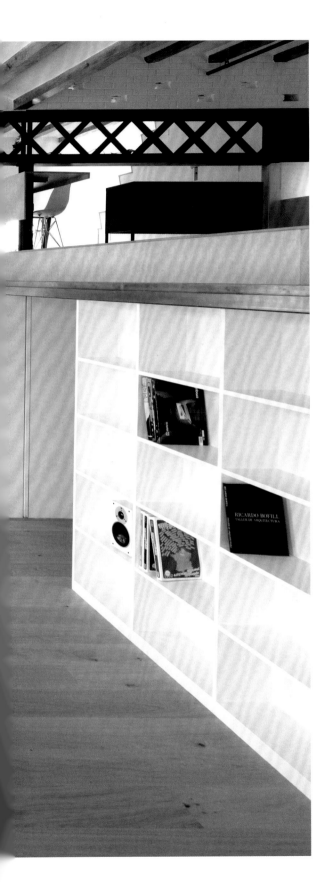

GROBER
FACTORY LOFT

110 m² | 1,184.03 sq ft

———

META STUDIO

———

BARCELONA, SPAIN

———

© LLUÍS CARBONELL, AITOR ESTÉVEZ

In this remodel of an old textile factory, an attempt was made to preserve its natural spaciousness while still providing a certain level of privacy. The lower level consists of an area that is completely open, with the different environments being delineated by the use of different materials; and a night zone, with two bedrooms and a bath. The upper level, which directly overlooks the lower, holds an office, a bathroom, and a sitting room.

Hier sehen Sie die Umgestaltung einer ehemaligen Textilfabrik. Die Bewohner möchten deren durchscheinende Natur bewahren und gleichzeitig ein gewisses Maß an Privatsphäre genießen. Im Erdgeschoss stoßen wir auf einen völlig offenen Bereich, in dem die Räume durch die verschiedenen hier eingesetzten Materialien abgegrenzt werden, und einen Schlafbereich, der aus zwei Schlafzimmern und einem Bad besteht. Die obere Etage ist optisch direkt mit der unteren Etage verbunden und umfasst ein Büro, ein Bad und ein Wohnzimmer.

Réaménagement d'une ancienne usine de textile. On a souhaité conserver la nature ouverte tout en souhaitant avoir un certain degré d'intimité. Au rez-de-chaussée se trouve un espace entièrement ouvert où les pièces sont délimitées par les divers matériaux utilisés, avec un espace nuit qui comprend deux chambres et une salle de bains. L'étage supérieur est en connexion visuelle directe avec l'étage inférieur et comprend un bureau, une salle de bains et un salon.

Remodelación de una antigua fábrica textil. Se quiere conservar su naturaleza diáfana a la vez que se desea tener un cierto grado de intimidad. En la planta baja nos encontramos con una zona completamente abierta, donde los ambientes están delimitados por los diferentes materiales utilizados, y con una zona de noche, que consiste en dos habitaciones y un baño. La planta superior, está en conexión visual directa con la inferior y contiene una oficina, un cuarto de baño y un salón.

The work area is on the mezzanine floor overlooking the space below. It has a bathroom and can be turned into a guest room if needed.

Der Arbeitsbereich ist im Zwischengeschoss angesiedelt, das zum unteren Raum hin offen ist und über ein Bad verfügt. Bei Bedarf kann es in ein Gästezimmer umgewandelt werden.

L'espace travail se trouve au niveau de la mezzanine au-dessus de l'espace inférieur qui dispose d'une salle de bains et peut se transformer en chambre d'amis si nécessaire.

La zona de trabajo está en el altillo, abierto sobre el espacio inferior, que dispone de un baño y puede convertirse en habitación de invitados en caso de necesidad.

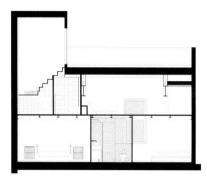

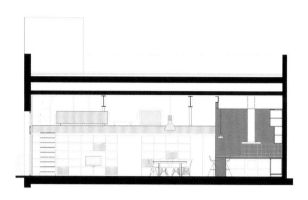

Longitudinal sections

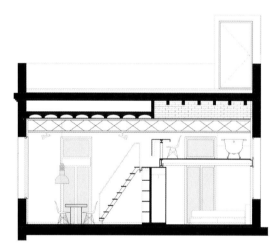

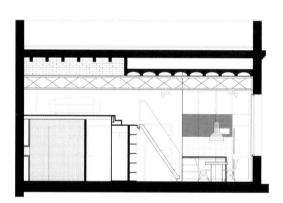

Cross sections

By using the enclosed room under the mezzanine for sleep, while also leaving the mezzanine open to the room below, the space is used as efficiently as possible without losing the feeling of openness.

Durch die Ausnutzung des geschlossenen Raumes unter dem Zwischengeschoss als Ruhebereich, wobei er zur unteren Etage hin offen bleibt, erreicht der Planer eine maximale Ausnutzung des Raumes ohne dabei Geräumigkeit zu verlieren.

Grâce à l'exploitation de l'espace fermé en dessous de la mezzanine comme zone de repos tout en laissant celui-ci ouvert sur l'étage inférieur, on a maximisé l'espace dans perdre en volume.

Gracias al aprovechamiento del espacio cerrado bajo el altillo como zona de descanso, pero dejando éste abierto sobre la planta inferior, se consigue un aprovechamiento máximo del espacio sin perder amplitud.

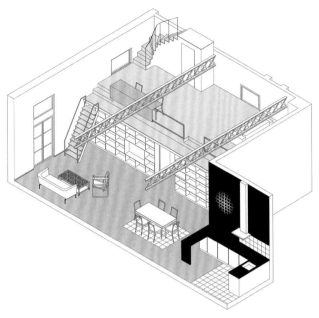

Axonometric view

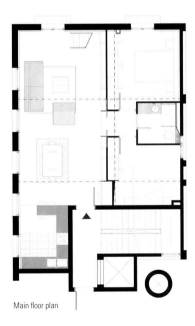

Main floor plan

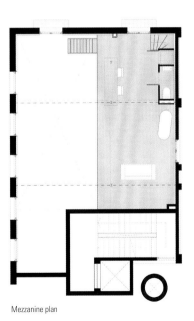

Mezzanine plan

One of the client's requirements was that there be a somewhat private sleeping area. This was achieved by siting the bedroom and bathroom under the mezzanine, and separating them from the main space with a bookcase.

Eine der Anforderungen des Kunden war, ein Ruhebereich mit einer gewissen Privatsphäre zu schaffen, was durch die Platzierung von Schlafzimmer und Bad im Zwischengeschoss erreicht wird, vom Hauptbereich mithilfe eines Bücherregals abgetrennt.

Une des exigences du client était de conserver un espace de détente avec une certaine intimité, ce que l'on a obtenu en plaçant la chambre et la salle de bain en dessous de la mezzanine, séparées de l'espace de vie par une bibliothèque.

Uno de los requisitos del cliente fue mantener una zona de descanso con una cierta intimidad, lo que se consiguó ubicándo el dormitorio y el baño bajo el altillo, separados de la zona principal mediante una biblioteca.

DIAPHANOUS INDUSTRIAL LOFT

115 m² | 237.85 sq ft

––––––

MARTIN ARCHITECTS

––––––

KIEV, UKRAINE

––––––

© IGOR KARPENKO

In a new downtown building, the architects designed this loft, which is characterized by the visibility of the original construction details. The interior features exposed bricks and beams, original factory windows, and a dark, stained wooden floor. The transparency they created among the spaces allows the light to circulate freely and provides a sense of space; the tradeoff, however, is a certain loss of privacy.

In einem Neubau im Stadtzentrum haben Architekten diesen Loft geschaffen, der sich dadurch auszeichnet, dass er den Baukomponenten der Wohnstätte Sichtbarkeit verleiht. Im Innenraum spielen unverputzte Backsteinwände, freigelegte Balken, Fenster aus Glas der Fabrik und dunkel gefleckte Holzböden die Hauptrolle. Die zwischen den Räumen geschaffene Transparenz ermöglicht, dass das Licht unbehindert zirkuliert, was der Wohnstätte ein Gefühl von Raum verleiht, obwohl deshalb auf eine gewisse Privatsphäre verzichtet werden musste.

Dans un bâtiment neuf du centre-ville, les architectes ont créé ce loft qui se caractérise par la visibilité des détails de construction du bien. Les murs en brique visible sont l'élément principal de l'intérieur, ainsi que les poutres apparentes, les fenêtres en verre de l'usine et les sols en bois foncé sali. La transparence créée entre les espaces permet à la lumière de circuler librement avec la sensation d'espace dans le loft, même si cela signifie renoncer à une certaine intimité.

En un nuevo edificio del centro de la ciudad, los arquitectos han creado este loft que se caracteriza por dar visibilidad a los detalles constructivos de la vivienda. Los interiores tienen como protagonista paredes de ladrillo visto, vigas al descubierto, ventanas de vidrio de la fábrica y suelos de madera oscura manchada. La transparencia creada entre los espacios permite que circule la luz libremente añadiendo sensación de espacio a la vivienda, aunque signifique renunciar a cierta privacidad.

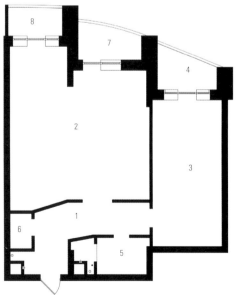

1. Corridor/Hallway
2. Kitchen/Living room
3. Bedroom
4. Loggia
5. Bathroom
6. Toilet
7. Loggia
8. Loggia

Plan before intervention

1. Corridor/Hallway
2. Kitchen/Living room
3. Bedroom
4. Dressing room
5. Bathroom
6. Toilet
7. Cabinet

Plan after intervention

The project eliminates certain walls so that the rooms appear to flow from one side to the other, thus creating continuity among the separate spaces.

Beim Umbau wurden einige Wände entfernt, wodurch der Eindruck entsteht, dass die Zimmer von einer Seite zur anderen fließen, was den verschiedenen Wohnbereichen Kontinuität verleiht.

Les travaux ont permis de retirer certains murs de sorte que les chambres paraissent s'échapper d'un côté à l'autre procurant de la continuité aux divers espaces.

En la reforma, se han eliminado algunas paredes de tal forma que las habitaciones parecen fluir de un lado al otro, dando continuidad a los distintos espacios.

This is also designed to be a "smart," completely automated dwelling; all the commands can be run from the owner's personal telephone.

Zudem ist die Wohnung als „Smart Home" konzipiert und umfassend mit Haustechnik ausgestattet, so dass alle Befehle vom Privathandy des Eigentümers aus erteilt werden können.

Le loft est également conçu comme une maison intelligente, parfaitement domotique, dans lequel toutes les commandes peuvent être exécutées depuis le téléphone personnel du propriétaire.

La vivienda también está concebida como una casa inteligente, perfectamente domotizada, en la que y todos los comandos pueden ser ejecutados desde el teléfono personal del propietario.

The glass divider that separates the sleeping area from the living area, along with the large picture window, allows the light to flood the entire abode, increasing the sense of spaciousness.

Neben einem großen Fenster zur Außenseite hin sorgt die Glaswand, die den Ruhebereich vom Wohnbereich trennt, dafür, dass das Licht in die ganze Wohnung einströmt, was den Wohnräumen Geräumigkeit verleiht.

Le grand paravent en verre qui sépare la chambre du séjour, avec une grande baie vitrée extérieure, permet à la lumière d'inonder tout le loft, donnant de la grandeur aux espaces.

La mampara acristalada que separa la zona de descanso de la zona de estar, junto con un gran ventanal exterior, permiten que la luz inunde toda la vivienda, dotando los espacios de gran amplitud.

LIGHT-FILLED DUPLEX

120 m² | 1,291.67 sq ft

‒‒‒‒

AXIS MUNDI / JOHN BECKMANN, NICK MESSERLIAN AND RICHARD ROSENBLOOM

‒‒‒‒

NEW YORK, NEW YORK, UNITED STATES

‒‒‒‒

© MIKIKO KIKUYAMA

It was an enormous challenge to condense all the functions of a home into this one-room space. However, because of the high ceiling, it was possible to lay it out on two levels. On the first floor can be found the kitchen and a generous living/dining space, bathed in natural light. A staircase leads to the bedroom on the second floor, which is the relaxation zone. The colors of the furniture, the decor, and the accessories are especially selected to enliven the overall architectural articulation.

Es war eine enorme Herausforderung, alle Funktionalitäten einer Wohnstätte in diesem aus einem Zimmer bestehenden Raum zu kondensieren. Die Deckenhöhe wurde ausgenutzt, um den Raum auf zwei Ebenen zu gliedern. Im unteren Teil befinden sich die Küche und ein großzügiges Wohn-Esszimmer, das von Tageslicht durchflutet wird. Eine Treppe ermöglicht den Zugang zum Zimmer auf der oberen Etage, wo sich der Ruhebereich befindet. Die Farbe von Mobiliar, Einrichtungsgegenständen und Accessoires wurden eigens ausgewählt, um die gesamte architektonische Artikulation zu beleben.

Cela a été un véritable défi de concentrer toutes les fonctionnalités d'une habitation dans un cet espace d'une seule chambre. On a su tirer profit de la hauteur sous plafond pour la réorganiser sur deux niveaux. Au rez-de-chaussée se trouvent la cuisine et un vaste salon-salle à manger baigné de lumière naturelle. Un escalier permet d'accéder à la chambre de l'étage supérieur où se trouve l'espace de détente. La couleur des meubles, la décoration et les accessoires ont été choisis avec soins afin d'égayer toute l'articulation architectonique.

Ha sido todo un reto condensar todas las funcionalidades de una vivienda en este espacio de una sola habitación. Se ha aprovechado la altura de techo para organizarla en dos niveles. En la parte inferior encontramos la cocina y un amplio salón-comedor bañado de luz natural. Una escalera permite acceso a la habitación en la planta superior, donde se ubica la zona descanso. El color de los muebles, la decoración y los accesorios son especialmente escogidos para animar toda la articulación arquitectónica.

The steel staircase leading to the upper room is attached to a side wall so that it takes up as little space as possible.

Die Stahltreppe, die zum Raum in der oberen Etage führt, hängt an der Seitenwand, um den Raum so wenig wie möglich zu schmälern.

L'escalier en acier qui mène à la chambre du niveau supérieur est suspendu au mur latéral pour retirer le plus petit espace possible.

La escalera de acero que lleva a la habitación en la planta superior, está colgada en la pared lateral para restar el menor espacio posible.

Panels of frosted glass partition off the upper mezzanine; they allow light into the bedroom, while providing privacy for the residents.

Um das Licht in das gesamte Zimmer fließen zu lassen und gleichzeitig die Privatsphäre des Eigentümers zu schützen, ist das Geländer der oberen Etage aus Mattglas.

Pour permettre à la lumière de pénétrer toute la chambre en protégeant l'intimité du propriétaire, la barrière de l'étage supérieur est en verre à l'émeri.

Para permitir que la luz llegue a toda la habitación y a la vez proteger la intimidad propietario, la barandilla del piso superior es de vidrio esmerilado.

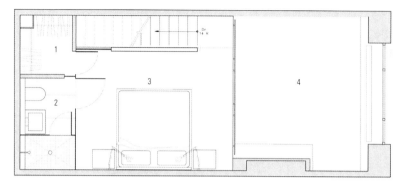

Mezzanine plan

1. Closet
2. Bathroom 2
3. Bedroom
4. Open to below

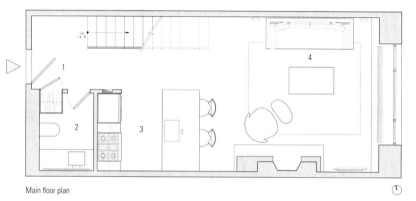

Main floor plan

1. Entry
2. Bathroom1
3. Kitchen
4. Living room

In this luminous loft, with its white walls and hardwood floors, the only remnant of the previous flat is the enormous arched window.

In diesem hellen Loft mit weißen Wänden und Holzböden, ist ein großes Bogenfenster das einzige Element, das von der vorherigen Wohnung übrigblieb.

Dans ce loft lumineux aux murs blancs et aux sols en bois, le seul élément qui reste du précédent appartement est la grande baie vitrée en forme d'arc.

En este luminoso loft de paredes blancas y suelos de madera, lo único que permanece del piso anterior es el gran ventanal en forma de arco.

OKUME HOME

120 m² | 1,291.67 sq ft

—

PAOLA MARÉ (INTERIOR DESIGNER) & RAIMONDO GUIDACCI (ARCHITECT)

—

TURIN, ITALY

—

© JANA SEBESTOVA

A former carpentry shop located in a courtyard is transformed into a modern loft. The lower floor contains the kitchen and the wood-encased main bathroom. The wall of the case that faces the kitchen becomes a storage space. Behind the sofa is a bookcase made of wood and iron; its lowest shelf continues along the wall to make a long bench. The multi-functional upper level holds the bedroom and an exposed bath tub.

Eine in einem Innenhof befindliche ehemalige Zimmerei wird in einen modernen Loft umgewandelt. Auf der unteren Etage finden wir die Küche und das große Bad, das sich in einem Holzkasten befindet. Die Wand des Kastens, die der Küche zugewandt ist, dient als Stauraum. Hinter dem Sofa steht ein Bücherregal aus Holz und Eisen, dessen unteres Regal an der Wand entlang fortfährt und eine lange Bank bildet. Der Raum in der oberen Etage dient als Multifunktionsbereich und beherbergt das Schlafzimmer mit einer Badewanne in Sichtweite.

Une ancienne menuiserie située dans une cour qui a été transformée en un loft moderne. Au rez-de-chaussée se trouvent la cuisine et la principale salle de bains située dans une caisse en bois. La paroi de la caisse qui donne sur la cuisine sert d'espace de rangement. Derrière le canapé se trouve une bibliothèque faite en bois et en métal dont l'étagère inférieure traverse le mur formant ainsi un long banc. L'espace de l'étage supérieur sert de zone multifonctionnelle comprenant la chambre avec une baignoire à vue.

Una vieja carpintería ubicada en un patio se transforma en un moderno loft. En la planta inferior encontramos la cocina y el baño principal, ubicado en una caja de madera. La pared de la caja que da a la cocina sirve como espacio de almacenaje. Detrás del sofá, encontramos una librería hecha de madera y hierro, cuyo estante inferior continúa por la pared formando un largo banco. El espacio de la planta superior sirve como área multifuncional, albergando el dormitorio con una bañera a la vista.

Tall windows run along the entire length of the first floor, which is the day zone; the light takes center stage and floods the entire space.

Große Fenster erstrecken sich über die gesamte Länge der unteren Etage, wo sich sämtliche Aufenthaltsbereiche befinden. Das Licht wird zur Hauptfigur und durchflutet den gesamten Raum.

De grandes baies vitrées parcourent toute la longueur de l'étage inférieur où se trouvent tous les espaces de vie. La lumière devient l'élément majeur et inonde tout l'espace.

Unos grandes ventanales cubren toda la longitud de la planta inferior, donde se encuentran todas las zonas de día; la luz se convierte en protagonista e inunda todo el espacio.

A substantial part of the flooring in the upper level is made of glass; this connects it visually with the lower floor and brings in the light from below. This gives continuity and spaciousness to the entire abode.

Ein Teil des Bodens der oberen Etage ist eine große verglaste Fläche, die sie optisch mit der unteren Etage verbindet und dafür sorgt, dass das Licht zirkuliert, das dort entstammt, was der gesamten Wohnstätte Kontinuität und Geräumigkeit verleiht.

Une partie du sol de l'étage supérieur est un grand espace en verre qui le relie visuellement à l'étage inférieur et permet ainsi à la lumière qui provient de celle-ci de circuler, conférant continuité et grandeur à tout le loft.

Parte del suelo de la planta superior es una gran zona acristalada que la conecta visualmente a con la planta inferior y permite que circule la luz que proviene de esta, lo que da continuidad y amplitud a toda la vivienda.

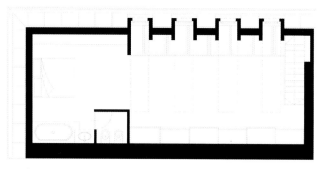

Second floor plan

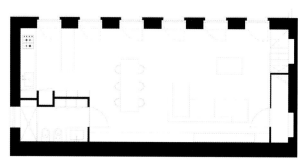

Ground floor plan

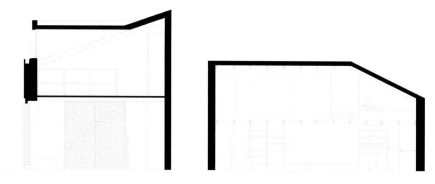

Sections

LOFT IN
LE PRÉ SAINT GERVAIS

130 m² | 1,399 sq ft

⁓⁓⁓⁓⁓

BARBARA STERKERS

⁓⁓⁓⁓⁓

LE PRÉ SAINT GERVAIS, FRANCE

⁓⁓⁓⁓⁓

© DAVID GILLES

This loft was created in the space formerly occupied by a factory. Because the central room had only one window, it was necessary to create more openings to the outside to add a sense of spaciousness to the living room. The polished glass ceilings over the bathrooms and the living room stairs help highlight the play of the natural light that circulates throughout. The color white, used on all the surfaces, including the floor, walls, and trim, heightens the sense of airiness.

Dieser Loft wurde in dem Raum erstellt, der einst eine Fabrik beherbergte. Im zentralen Wohnbereich gab es nur ein Fenster, weshalb es notwendig war, mehr Öffnungen nach außen hin zu schaffen, um dem Wohnzimmer ein Gefühl von Geräumigkeit zu geben. Das Mattglas, das die Bäder oder die Treppe des Wohnzimmers bedeckt, trägt dazu bei, das Spiel des Tageslichtes zu verstärken, das im Haus zirkuliert. Die weiße Farbe an allen Oberflächen, sowie an Boden, Wänden und Holzarbeiten, verstärkt das Gefühl von Durchsichtigkeit der Wohnstätte.

Ce loft a été créé dans un espace où se trouvait autrefois une ancienne usine. La partie centrale n'avait qu'une fenêtre, par conséquent il a été nécessaire de créer davantage d'ouvertures sur l'extérieur afin de donner la sensation de grandeur à la pièce. Le verre poli qui couvre les salles de bains ou les escaliers du séjour contribue à renforcer le jeu de lumière naturelle qui circule dans le loft. La couleur blanche de toutes les surfaces, ainsi que le sol, les murs et la boiserie renforcent la sensation de transparence du loft.

Este loft ha sido creado en el espacio que ocupaba una antigua fábrica. En el ambiente central solo había una ventana, con lo que es necesario crear más aperturas al exterior para dar sensación de amplitud a la sala. El vidrio pulido que cubre los baños y las escaleras de la sala de estar contribuye a reforzar el juego de luz natural que circula en la casa. El color blanco en todas las superficies, así como el suelo, paredes y carpintería, refuerza la sensación de diafanidad de la vivienda.

The refurbished iron beams crossing the space
were once part of the original construction.
They are among the key features of this loft,
as they have a look that is simultaneously
industrial and modern.

Die aus dem früheren Bau stammenden
und renovierten Eisenträger, die den Raum
durchkreuzen, sind eines der Schlüsselelemente
dieses Lofts, und verleihen ihm gleichzeitig ein
modernes Aussehen mit Industriecharakter.

Les poutres métalliques qui parcourent
l'espace, reprises de l'ancienne construction,
sont des éléments majeurs dans ce loft lui
donnant un air à la fois industriel et moderne.

Las vigas de hierro que recorren el espacio,
reformadas de la anterior construcción, son
uno de los elementos protagonistas de este
loft dotándolo de un aire a la vez industrial
y moderno.

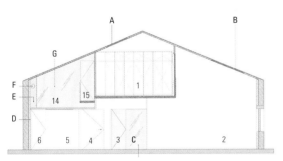

Section A-A

A. Laminated glazing/tempered
Thermal summer/winter + anti
intrusion
B. Canopy opening 5240 x 1950 mm
Metal frame
Laminated glazing/tempered
Thermal summer/winter + anti
intrusion
C. Translucid glass
D. Wall insulation
Vapor barrier
Rockwool + BA13
E. Stainless steel plate with cutout
for VMC
F. VMC
G. Translucid glass

1. Room 2
2. Living room
3. Bathroom
4. Cellar
5. Utility room
6. WC
14. Bathroom
15. Catwalk

Section B-B

A. VMC
B. Wall insulation vapor barrier
rockwool + BA13
C. Metal frame
D. Canopy opening 5240 x 1950 mm
Metal frame
Laminated glazing/tempered
Thermal summer/winter + anti
intrusion

1. Room 1
2. Catwalk
3. Office
4. Dressing entry
5. Kitchen
6. Living room

An iron staircase leading to the upper level is a perfect match for the metal structure of the roof beams, and helps achieve visual continuity between the two spaces.

Der Zugang zum oberen Bereich erfolgt mithilfe der Eisentreppe, die perfekt zum Metallgefüge der Deckenbalken passt, wodurch eine visuelle Kontinuität zwischen beiden Räumen erzielt wird.

L'accès à l'étage supérieur se fait part un escalier métallique qui se combine parfaitement à la structure métallique des poutres du plafond, offrant ainsi une continuité visuelle entre les deux espaces.

El acceso a la zona superior se realiza mediante una escalera de hierro, que combina perfectamente con la estructura metálica de las vigas del techo, logrando una continuidad visual entre los dos espacios.

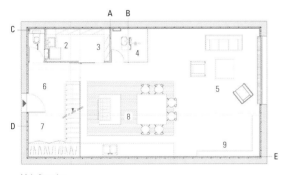

Main floor plan

A. Partition placostyle 7 cm
B. Translucid glass
C. Evacuation
   Water level
D. Wall insulation
   Vapor barrier
   Rockwool + BA13
E. Evacuation

1. Toilet
2. Utility room
3. Cellar
4. Bathroom
5. Living room
6. Entrance
7. Dressing entry storage
8. Dining room/Kitchen
9. Library

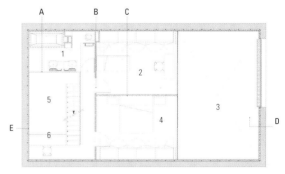

Mezzanine plan

A. Translucid glass
B. Isopplane door
C. Isophonic partition
   placostyle 7 cm
D. Metal gantry
E. Wall insulation
   Vapor barrier
   Rockwool + BA13

1. Bathroom
2. Room 2
3. Empty space over
   the living room
4. Room 1
5. Empty space over
   the entrance
6. Office

LOFT FULL
OF ART

130 m² | 1,399.31 sq ft

——

KAYSERSTUDIO

——

BARCELONA, SPAIN

——

© CECILIA MOTA

This loft, located on the second-highest floor of a '70s industrial building in Barcelona's Poblenou district, first attracted its owners because of its outdoor terrace with views of the sea. It was remodeled to open up the facade as much as possible to create an open, experimental space, with its glass acting like large screen revealing scenes of the city. All the interior walls were demolished to create one open area; thus, by using only concrete columns and items of furniture to delineate the different rooms, a sense of spaciousness is achieved.

Dieses Loft ist auf der vorletzten Etage eines Industriegebäudes aus den 70-er Jahren im Stadtbezirk Poblenou angesiedelt, und dessen Inhaber verliebten sich in dessen Terrasse mit Blick aufs Meer. Bei der Umgestaltung wird die Fassade maximal geöffnet, um einen offenen und experimentellen Raum mit Glastüren wie eine Art großen Bildschirm auf die Stadt zu schaffen. Alle Innenwände wurden abgerissen, wodurch ein einziger durchscheinender Bereich entsteht, wobei das Mobiliar und die Säulen aus Beton die Räume abgrenzen und für ein großartiges Gefühl von Geräumigkeit sorgen.

Ce loft est situé à l'avant-dernier étage d'un bâtiment industriel des années 70 dans le quartier de Poblenou. Les propriétaires sont tombés amoureux de la terrasse extérieure avec vue sur la mer. Les travaux ont permis d'ouvrir la façade au maximum afin de créer un espace ouvert et expérimental avec des portes-fenêtres comme un grand écran sur la ville. Tous les murs intérieurs ont été supprimés pour créer un espace unique ouvert délimité par le mobilier et les colonnes en béton, ce qui confère une grande sensation de volume.

Ubicado en la penúltima planta de un edificio industrial de los años 70 en el barrio de Poblenou, los dueños de este loft se enamoraron de la terraza exterior con vistas al mar. En la reforma, se abre la fachada al máximo para crear un espacio abierto y experimental, con unas cristaleras como una gran pantalla sobre la ciudad. Se derriban todas las paredes interiores creando una única zona diáfana, siendo el mobiliario y las columnas de hormigón, los que delimitan los espacios, logrando una gran sensación de amplitud.

An eye-catching leather sofa is the central point of interest in the living room, which is completely open; it is separated from the bedroom behind it by only a wooden bookcase.

Ein auffälliges Ledersofa wird zum zentralen Element des Wohnbereichs, der ein vollständig durchscheinender Bereich ist, vom Schlafsaal nur durch ein Bücherregal aus Holz im hinteren Teil des Raumes abgetrennt.

Un canapé en cuir voyant devient l'élément phare du séjour entièrement ouvert, simplement séparé de la chambre par une bibliothèque en bois au fond de la salle.

Un vistoso sofá de piel se convierte en el elemento central de la zona de estar, que es un área completamente diáfana, separada del dormitorio tan solo por una librería de madera, al fondo de la sala.

The near-minimalist furniture with its straight lines, reaches its maximum effect in the kitchen/dining room. The loft, which is completely open to the outside, provides spectacular views of the city.

Das Mobiliar mit geraden Linien und fast minimalistisch geprägt erreicht seinen höchsten Ausdruck im Bereich Küche-Esszimmer. Der komplett nach außen offene Loft bietet eine spektakuläre Aussicht auf die Stadt.

Le mobilier, en ligne droite, et quasi minimaliste, atteint son expression maximale dans la cuisine-salle à manger. Le loft, entièrement ouvert sur l'extérieur, offre des vues spectaculaires de la ville.

El mobiliario, de líneas rectas, y casi minimalista, alcanza su máxima expresión en la cocina-comedor. El loft, completamente abierto al exterior, proporciona unas vistas espectaculares de la ciudad.

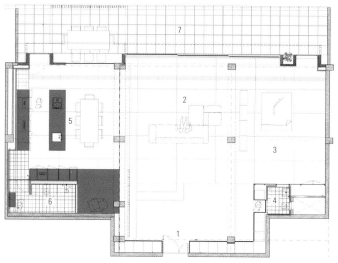

Floor plan

1. Entrance
2. Living room
3. Bedroom
4. Toilet
5. Dining room/Kitchen
6. Bathroom
7. Terrace

The leading roles in this loft are played by light and space. The use of low furniture, and the pale colors of the floors and walls, maximize the sense of spaciousness, so that it appears much larger than it actually is.

Licht und Raum sind die großen Protagonisten dieses Lofts. Der Einsatz niedriger Möbel und die hellen Farben an Boden und Wänden steigern das Gefühl von Geräumigkeit, wodurch der Loft viel größer erscheint, als er eigentlich ist.

La lumière et l'espace sont les éléments phares de ce loft. L'utilisation des meubles bas et les couleurs claires du sol et des murs amplifient la sensation de grandeur donnant ainsi l'impression d'un espace beaucoup plus grand qu'il n'y parait.

La luz y el espacio, son los grandes protagonistas de este loft. El uso de muebles bajos, y los colores claros del suelo y las paredes, magnifican la sensación de amplitud, logrando que parezca mucho más grande de lo que es.

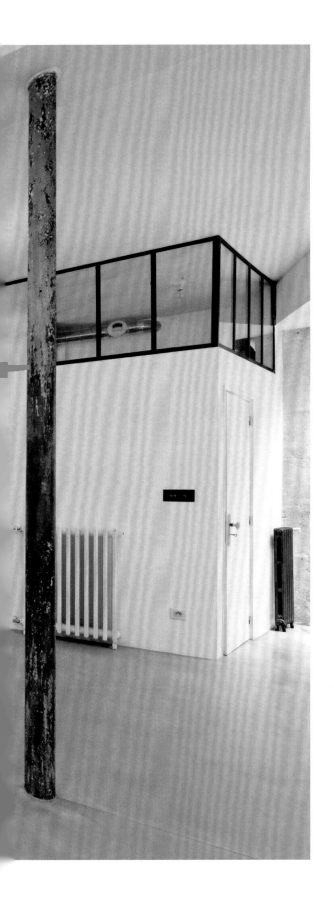

ATELIER CONVERTED INTO LOFT

130 m² | 1,399.31 sq ft

———

MAXIME JANSENS

———

PARIS, FRANCE

———

© CÉCILE SEPTET

The two courtyards, once occupied by an artisan workshop, have been completely roofed over to create an open space where the key elements are the roof, walls, and windows. The space right underneath the main skylight becomes a play space for children and/or a work space. The rest of the renovation focuses mainly on the finishes; top quality materials are selected, and then used in a simple way that expresses their intrinsic qualities.

Bei der Umgestaltung dieser Wohnstätte wurden zwei Innenhöfe, die als ehemaliges Atelier eines Kunsthandwerker dienten, überdacht, wodurch ein durchscheinender Raum geschaffen wurde, in dem das Tageslicht von Decke, Wänden und Fenstern eine Hauptrolle spielt. Der Bereich, der direkt unter dem Oberlicht liegt, dient als Spielbereich für die Kinder und zum Arbeiten. Der übrige Eingriff konzentriert sich hauptsächlich auf die Oberflächen: Hochwertige Materialien wurden ausgewählt, die auf einfache Weise eingesetzt werden, um ihre eigentlichen Qualitäten auszudrücken.

Les travaux de cette habitation concernent les deux cours qui forment un ancien atelier artisanal créant ainsi un espace ouvert dans lequel la lumière naturelle du plafond, des murs et fenêtres joue un rôle majeur. La partie qui se trouve juste en dessous de la lucarne principale sert d'aire de jeux pour les enfants et pour travailler. Le reste des travaux se focalise surtout sur les finitions : des matériaux de grande qualité utilisés de manière simple ont été choisis pour exprimer leurs qualités intrinsèques.

En la reforma de esta vivienda se cubren por completo los dos patios que formaban un antiguo taller artesano creando un espacio diáfano en el que la luz natural de techo, paredes y ventanas juega un papel protagonista. El área que se encuentra justo debajo de la claraboya principal sirve como zona de juegos para los niños y para trabajar. El resto de la intervención se centra sobre todo en los acabados: se seleccionan materiales de gran calidad que son usados de forma simple para expresar sus cualidades intrínsecas.

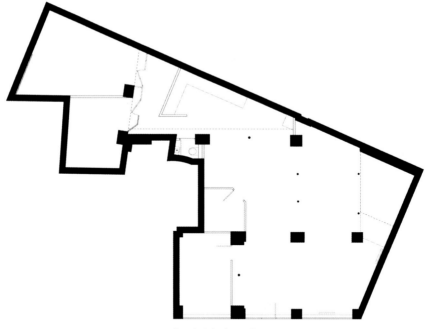

Floor plan before intervention

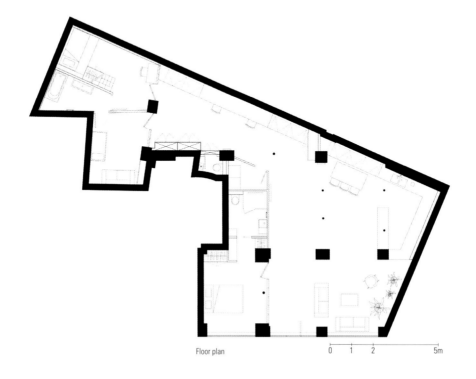

Floor plan

0 1 2   5m

The materials used are concrete, steel, and timber, deliberately left unfinished to express their intrinsic characteristics.

Die verwendeten Materialien sind absichtlich unbearbeiteter Beton, Stahl und unbearbeitetes Holz, um deren eigene Qualitäten zum Ausdruck zu bringen.

Les matériaux utilisés sont le béton, l'acier et le bois laissés délibérément bruts afin d'exprimer leurs propres qualités.

Los materiales empleados son hormigón, acero y madera deliberadamente dejados en bruto para expresar sus propias cualidades.

The interior is lit mostly by the skylights and by the outside windows.

Die Innenräume werden hauptsächlich durch die Oberlichter und die nach außen gehenden Fenster erhellt.

Les espaces intérieurs sont majoritairement éclairés par les lucarnes et les fenêtres donnant sur l'extérieur.

Los espacios interiores están mayoritariamente iluminados por las claraboyas y por las ventanas al exterior.

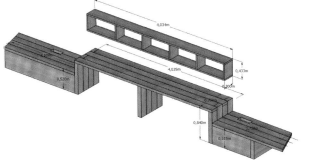

Perspective views of bench, bureau and shelves

There are few separate spaces in the loft, and glass walls have been created to foster the sense of spaciousness and allow for free circulation of light.

Die wenigen Trennungen dieses Lofts sind Glaswände, die das Gefühl von Geräumigkeit verstärken und dem Licht eine freie Zirkulation zu ermöglichen.

Pour les rares séparations du loft, des murs en verre ont été créés afin de renforcer la sensation de volume et laisser la lumière circuler librement.

En las pocas separaciones del loft, se crean paredes de cristal para reforzar la sensación de amplitud y para que circule la luz libremente.

DIRECTORY

Ambau Taller d'arquitectes
ambau.es
Valencia, Spain

Axis Mundi
axismundi.com
New York, New York, United States

Barbara Sterkers Architecte d'intérieur
barbara-sterkers.com
Paris, France

Beriot Bernardini Arquitectos
beriotbernardini.net
Madrid, Spain

De Goma
de-goma.com
Barcelona, Spain

Diego Revollo
diegorevollo.com.br
São Paulo, Brazil

Dröm Living
dromliving.com
Barcelona, Spain

Estudio de creación Josep Cano
osepcano.com
Barcelona, Spain

Falken Reynolds
alkenreynolds.com
Vancouver, British Columbia, Canada

Federico Delrosso Architects
federicodelrosso.com
Milan, Italy

G Architectcs Studio
g-archi.info
Tokyo, Japan

GK_Kayserstudio
kayserstudio.com
Barcelona, Spain

GutGut
gutgut.sk
Bratislava, Slovakia

In Arch - Interjero architekhtura
inarch.lt
Vilnius, Lithuania

Inblum
inblum.com
Vilnius, Lithuania

Kyu Sung Woo Architects
kswa.com
Cambridge, Massachusetts, United States

Loft Factory
loft-factory.com
Warsaw, Poland

LOT - Office for architecture
lot-arch.com
New York, New York, United States

Martin Architects
martins.com.ua
Kiev, Ukraine

Maxime Jansens Architecte
maximejansens.fr
Pantin, France

Meta Studio
meta-studio.eu
Barcelona, Spain
Paris, France

MIKOŁAJSKAstudio
mikolajskastudio.pl
Kraków, Poland

Mob Architects
mobarchitects.com
Rome, Italy

mode:lina architekci
modelina-architekci.com
Poznań, Poland

OOOOX
oooox.com
Prague, Czech Republic

Paola Maré
paolamare.it
Turin, Italy

Prisca Pellerin, Architecture et intérieur
priscapellerin.houzz.fr
Ivry-sur-Seine, France

R3 Architetti
r3architetti.com
Turin, Italy

RUE
soluciones espaciales
ruespace.com
Pamplona, Spain

SADAR+VUGA
sadarvuga.com
Ljubljana, Slovenia

Septembre Architecture
septembrearchitecture.com
Paris, France

Terra e Tuma
terraetuma.com.br
São Paulo, Brazil

Tim Diekhans Architektur
timdiekhans.squarespace.com
Bochum, Germany